Text research: Richard Ashby

Acknowledgements

This book would not have been possible without the help of many people at the university colleges and institutions included; I am grateful to them all. Special thanks go to Susan Marshall at Exeter College, Geoffrey Bourne-Taylor and Deborah Eaton at St Edmund Hall, Joanna Dodsworth at the Bodleian Library, the Botanic Garden and Oxford Central Library. Photographs of New College are by kind permission of the Warden and Fellows.

I particularly wish to thank Richard Ashby for his unfaltering commitment to this project. The following also gave their invaluable help and support: Professor Diarmaid MacCulloch and Mark Achurch, Robert Ashby, Angela Dixon, Robert Reddaway, Kenneth D. Smith, Margaret and Frank Turner, Donald Greig and, finally, Sarah Letts, Reina Ruis and all at Jarrold Publishing.

John Curtis

Front cover: Hertford Bridge (the 'Bridge of Sighs')
Back cover: Christ Church, hall

First published in 2000. Publication in this form © Pitkin 2019
43 Great Ormond Street,
London WC1N 3HZ

An imprint of B. T. Batsford Holdings Ltd

ISBN 978-1-84165-844-5

Printed by Dream Colour, China
2/26

A CIP catalogue for this book is available from the British Library.

This book can be ordered direct from the publisher at www.batsfordbooks.com, or try your local bookshop.

Distributed throughout the UK and Europe by Abrams & Chronicle Books, 1st Floor, 22–24 Ely Place, London EC1N 6TE and 57 rue Gaston Tessier, 75166 Paris, France
www.abramsandchronicle.co.uk
info@abramsandchronicle.co.uk

FSC www.fsc.org MIX Paper | Supporting responsible forestry FSC® C188448

Publisher's note Variant and archaic spellings have been retained in quoted material, while the modern spellings of place names have been used in headings. The inclusion of a photograph in this book does not necessarily imply public access to the building illustrated.

OXFORD

IN PICTURES

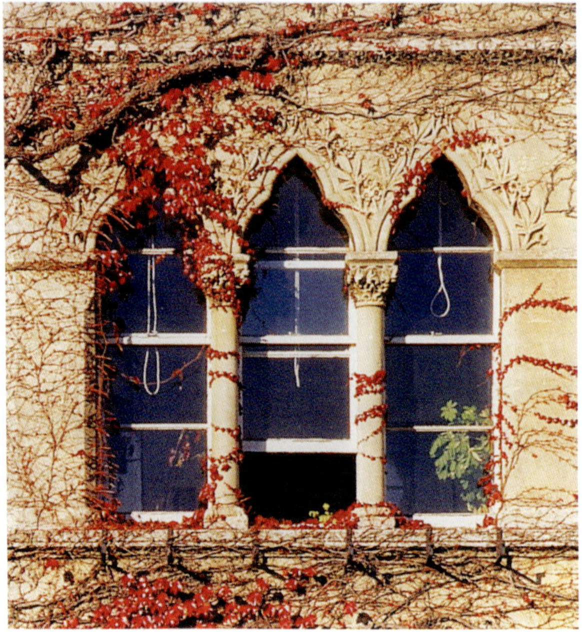

Christ Church, Meadow Buildings

OXFORD

IN PICTURES

PITKIN

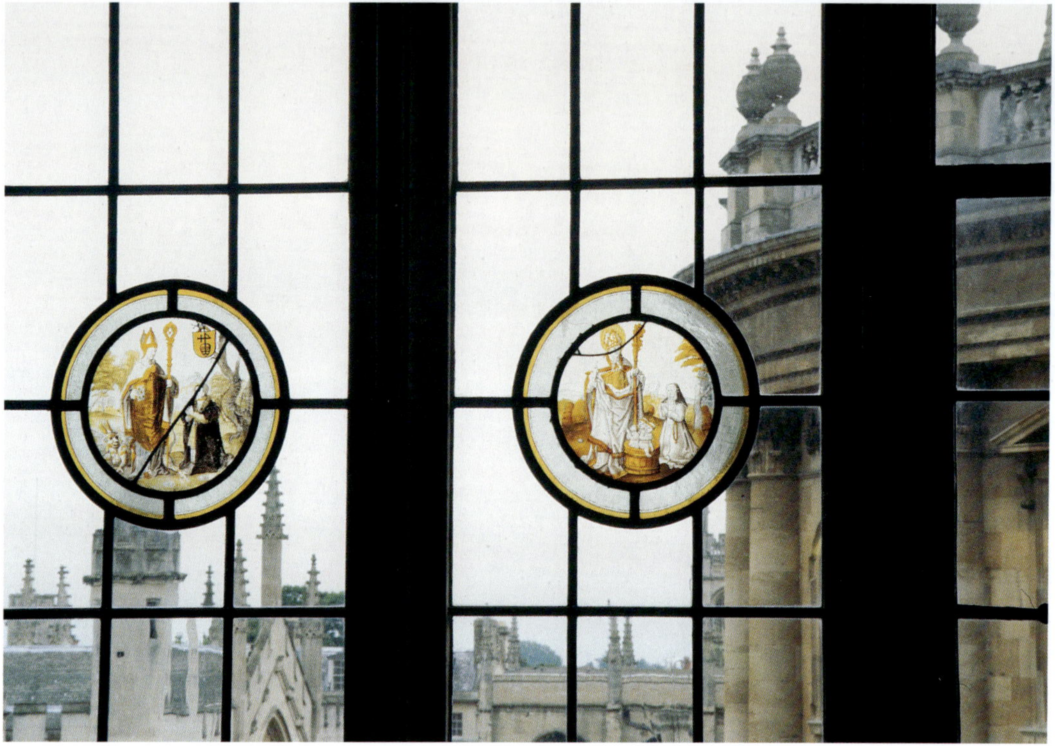

Bodleian Library

Contents

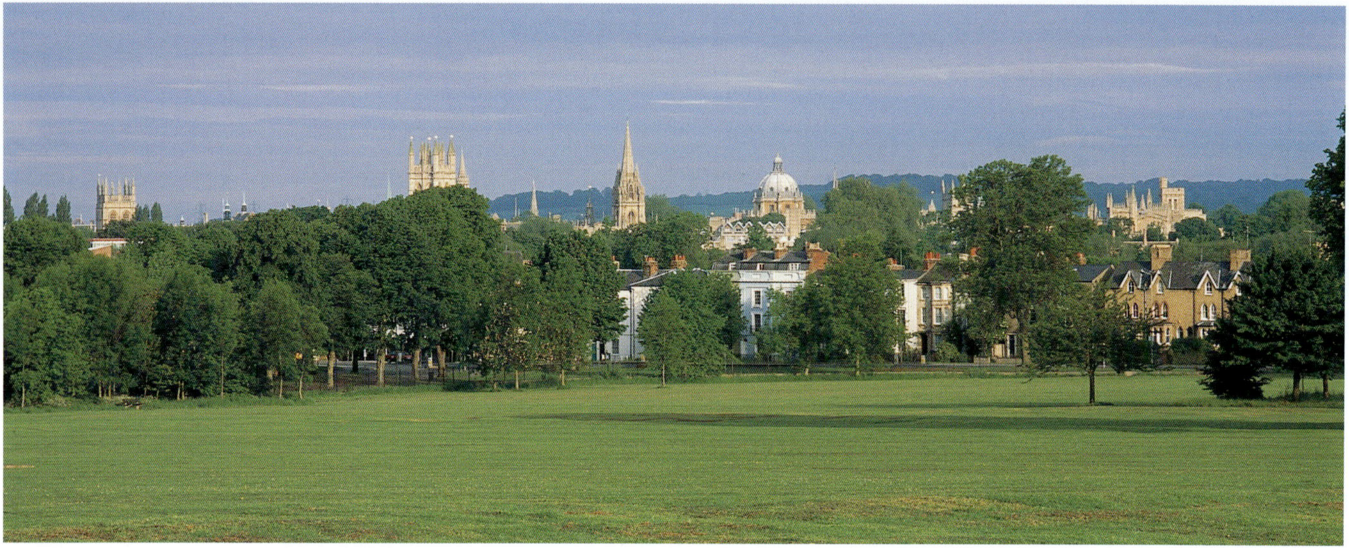

OXFORD FROM SOUTH PARK

The city of Oxford afforded us a very noble view on the road, and its spires, towers, and domes soon made me forget all the little objects of minor spleen that had been crossing me as I journeyed towards them ... their grandeur, nobility, antiquity, and elevation impressed my mind so forcibly ...

FANNY BURNEY *Diary* 1786

Introduction

I had been waiting in South Park for about half an hour before the sun eventually peered over the horizon. In an instant the chill of the early morning dissipated – shadows stretched across the glistening grass and down the slope towards the city, and the spires, towers and domes were bathed in the soft yellow light peculiar to mid-summer mornings. The camera shutter clicked and I had the first shot of the day.

Minutes later I was making my way down the hillside and into the already stirring town. The slender tower of Magdalen College appeared to glow in the hazy sun.

A short walk along The High, passing three young men, two immaculately dressed in dinner suits, the other painted green from his hair down to his shoes, brought me into Radcliffe Square where the spire of the Church of St Mary the Virgin and the dome of Radcliffe Camera looked particularly impressive amid the early morning calm.

On to the Sheldonian Theatre and then along Broad Street and into leafy St Giles. There was so much to photograph before the light became too harsh and the streets began to bustle with Oxford life.

Many mornings were spent this way during the year I recorded the images presented in this book. Oxford is an exceptional place: a city renowned for its university, its architecture and its colourful history. It is difficult to explore the ancient streets without feeling the presence of past artists, writers and poets, politicians, scientists, philosophers and clerics who were nurtured and inspired here. Days were filled choosing subjects for the camera lens, and with each day the town revealed a little more of itself.

Evenings were usually spent in a second rush of camera activity to make the most of the warm light on Oxford's many beautiful and historic buildings. The same day I had greeted the sunrise in South Park, I made my way south out of the city to catch the sun setting over the wide open space of Boars Hill. The day had grown uncomfortably hot and stuffy, but here the air was cool and fresh, and Oxford was clearly spread out before me, its spires glinting in the rich evening light. The camera shutter clicked – I took the last shot of the day.

JOHN CURTIS

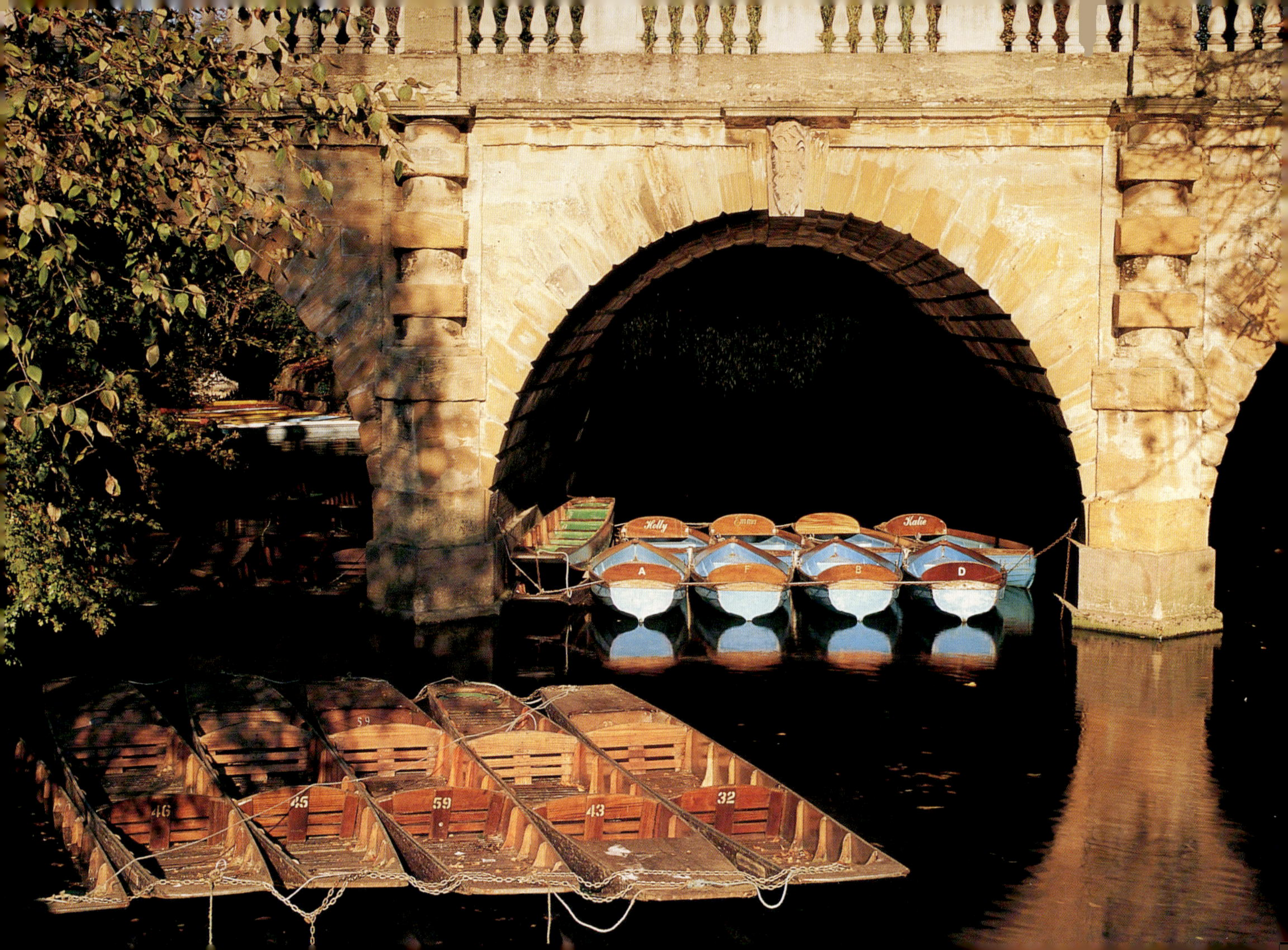
Holly
Katie
A
B
D
46
45
59
43
32

MAGDALEN BRIDGE

There is great store of boats of all kinds let out at very reasonable rates, and should his taste run in the direction of quiet rather than to the bustle and activity of the Isis, he may explore the winding Cherwell and, moored in his punt, watch

'Deep-bosomed in some cool retreat
The long reed grasses nod and greet
The stream that murmurs as it goes,'

or the flashing kingfisher as he darts on his prey.

Oxford Visitors and Entertainments Committee
Oxford
1915

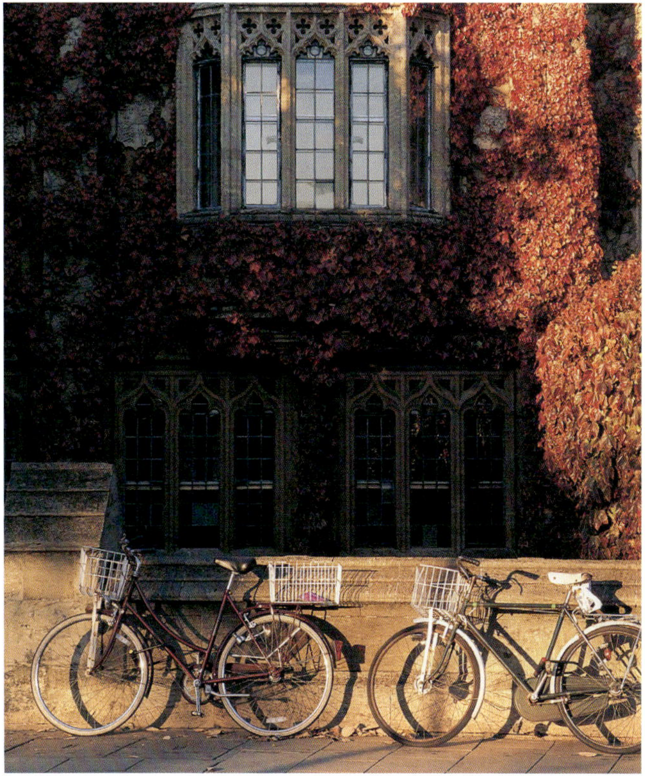

MAGDALEN COLLEGE

... my apartment consisted of three elegant and well furnished rooms in the new building, a stately pile, of Magdalen College.

Edward Gibbon
Memoirs of My Life and Writings
1796

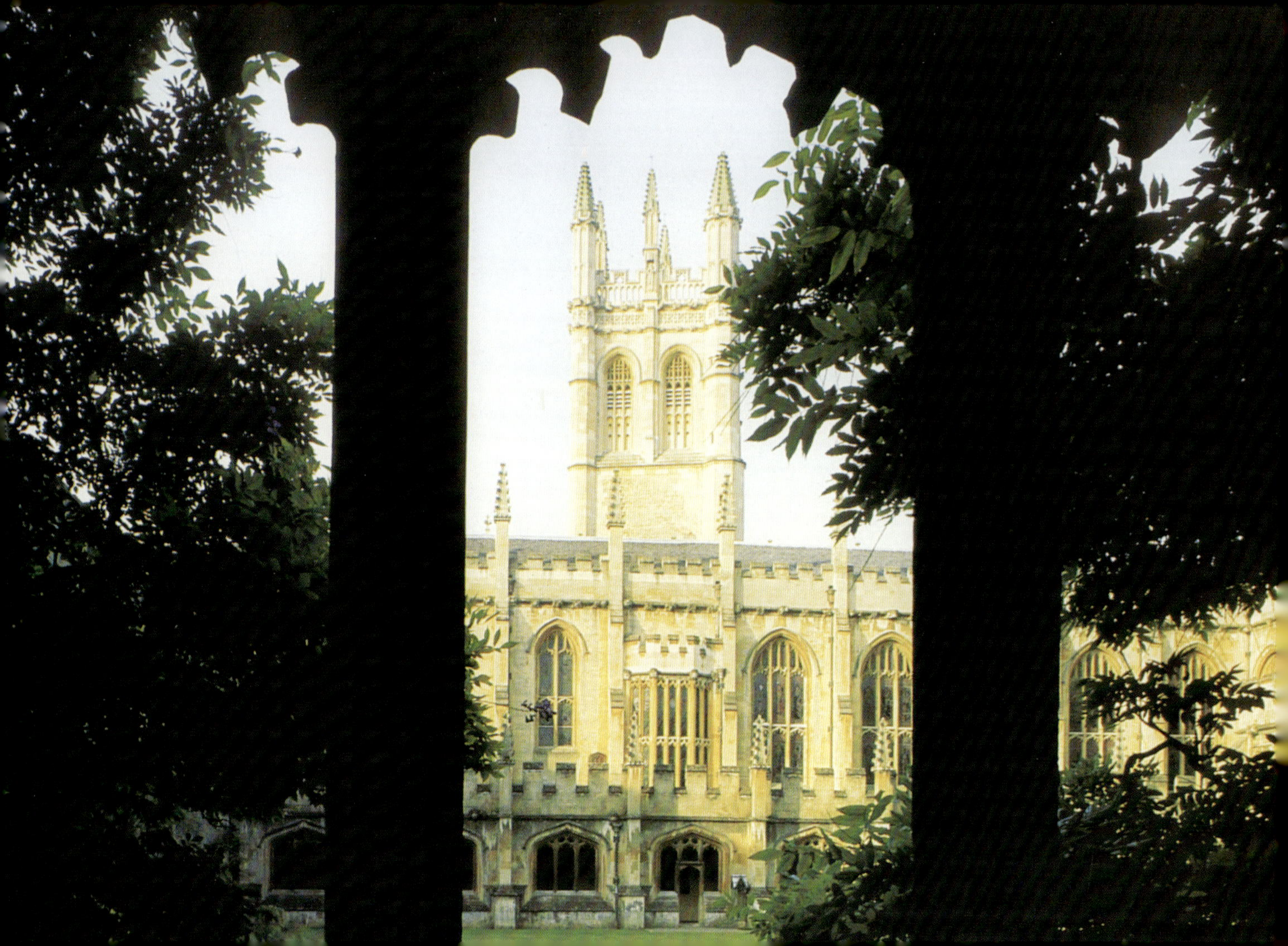

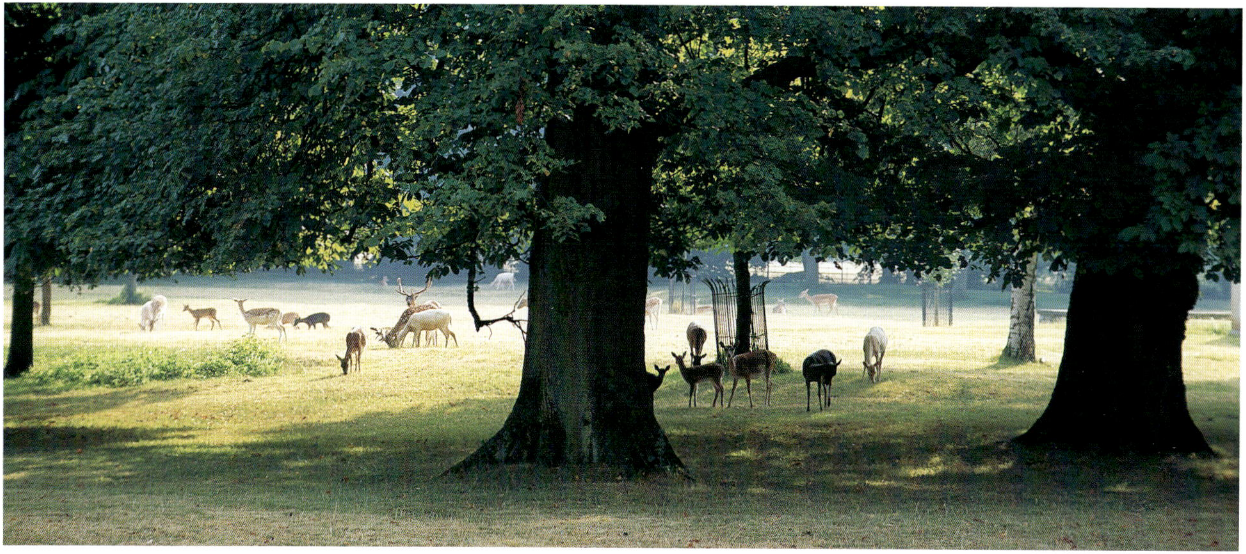

MAGDALEN COLLEGE The Cloister

… glees and madrigals were always sung at the top of this tower at sunrise on May morning to usher in the spring, but these have now given way to a hymn. On this occasion the bells (called … the most tuneable and melodious in all these parts) are all rung, when the whole tower shakes and bends perceptibly.

A Handbook for Travellers in Berks, Bucks, and Oxfordshire 1860

MAGDALEN COLLEGE Deer Park

Magdalen indeed with its deer park and its water walks combines the dignity of a college with the magnificence of a country seat.

Herbert A. Evans
Highways and Byways in Oxford and the Cotswolds 1905

MAGDALEN COLLEGE
Addison's Walk

In 1717 Merton College closed her garden 'on account of its being too much frequented by young scholars and ladies on Sunday nights. Thereupon the young gentlemen and others betook themselves to Magdalen Walk which is now every Sunday night in summer-time strangely filled just like a fair.'

Joanna Cannan
Oxfordshire
(County Books)
1952

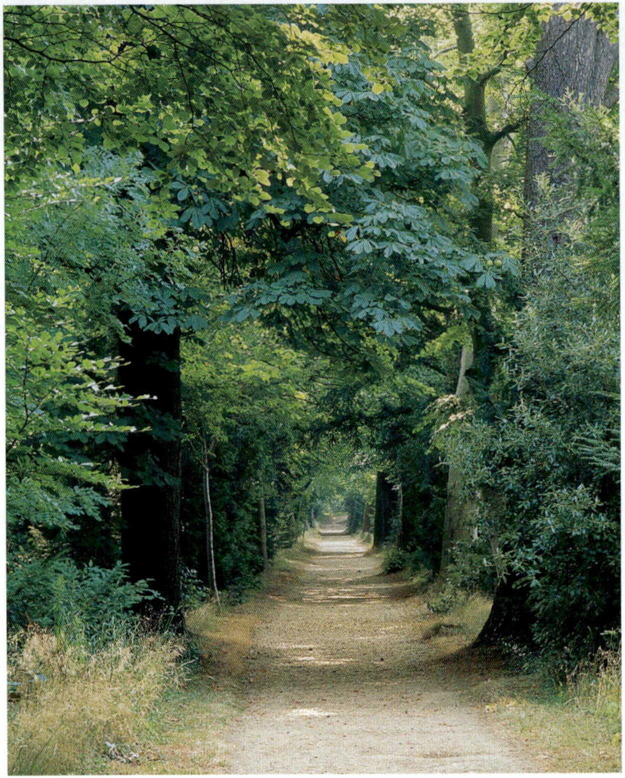

LONGWALL STREET
Former Garage of William Morris

At the age of 16, William Morris started repairing bicycles at his home in James Street and then bought and sold his own bicycles at a shop in the High Street. In August 1901 he moved his business to stables on Longwall Street, under the shadow of the old city walls, where he began repairing and hiring motor cars. When business increased, his landlord, Merton College, erected this building for him and here he built his first round-nosed 'Morris Oxford' car.

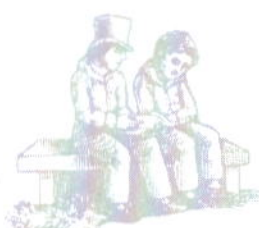

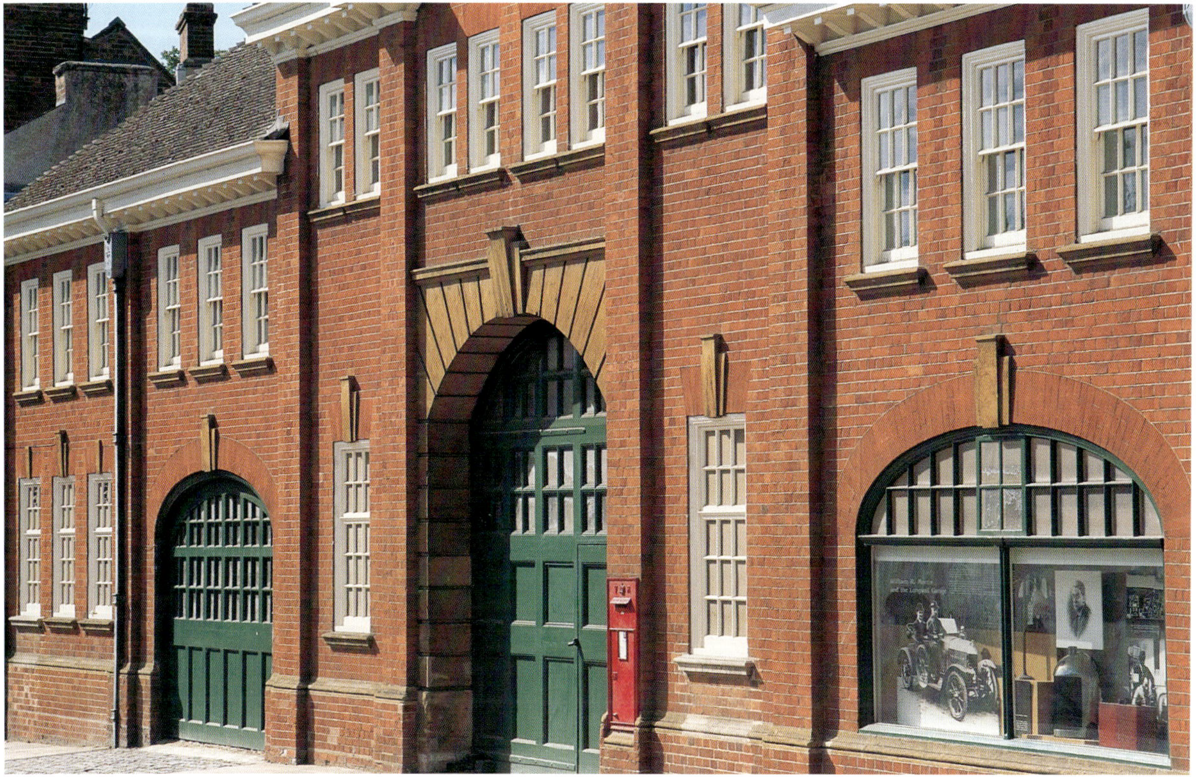

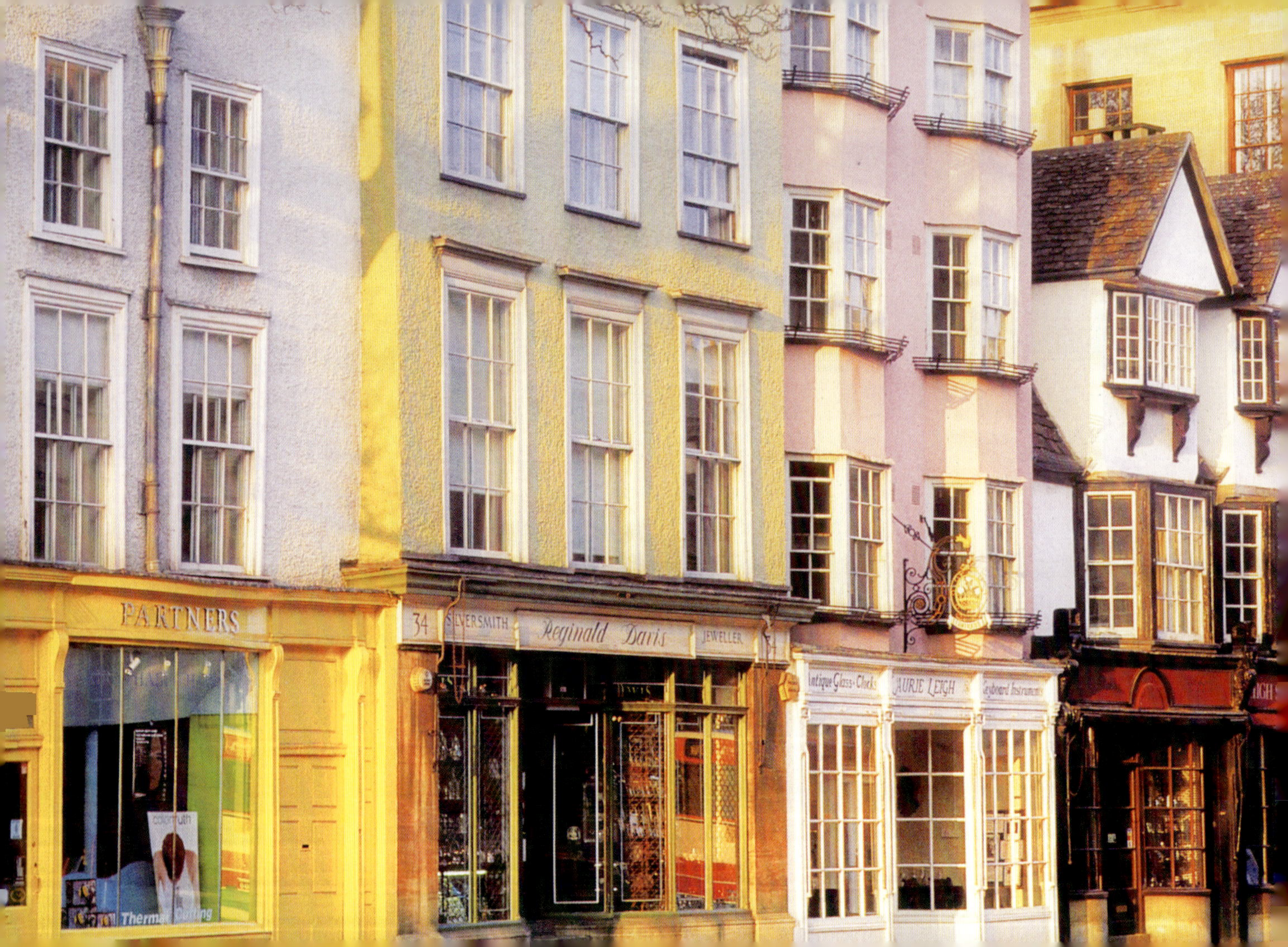
PARTNERS
34
SILVERSMITH
Reginald Davis
JEWELLER
Antique Glass · Clocks
AURIE LEIGH

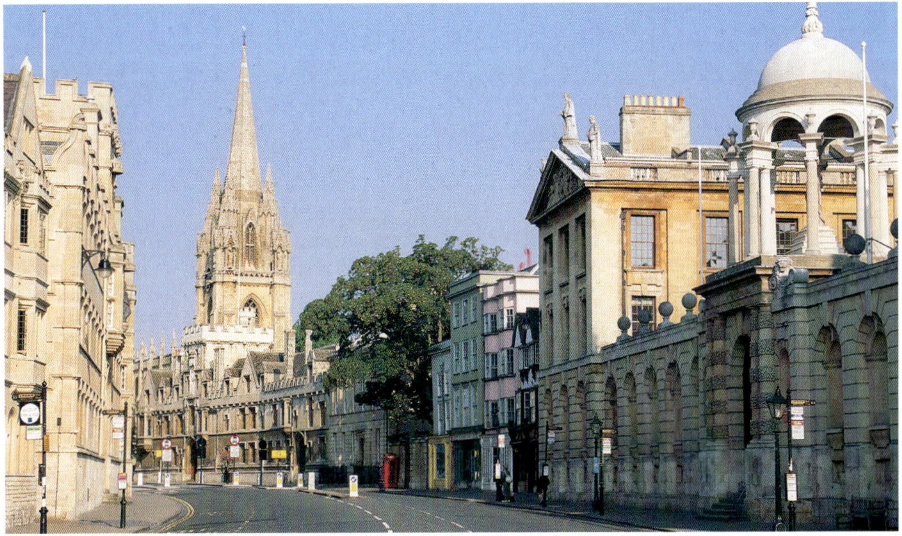

HIGH STREET

Oxymoron, a student magazine of the late 1960s, went into a paroxysm of excitement over a pair of flares: 'There is a male boutique …' it enthused. 'This fact, clearly the most important thing to happen in Oxford this century, does not seem to have attracted the attention it merits … You will be fascinated to know', continued the student journalist, 'that I have my eyes on some mauve cord trousers that are just fantastic. It's a gas, man …'.

PETER SNOW *Oxford Observed* 1991

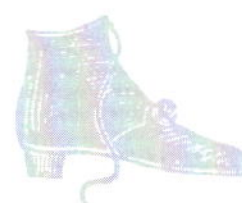

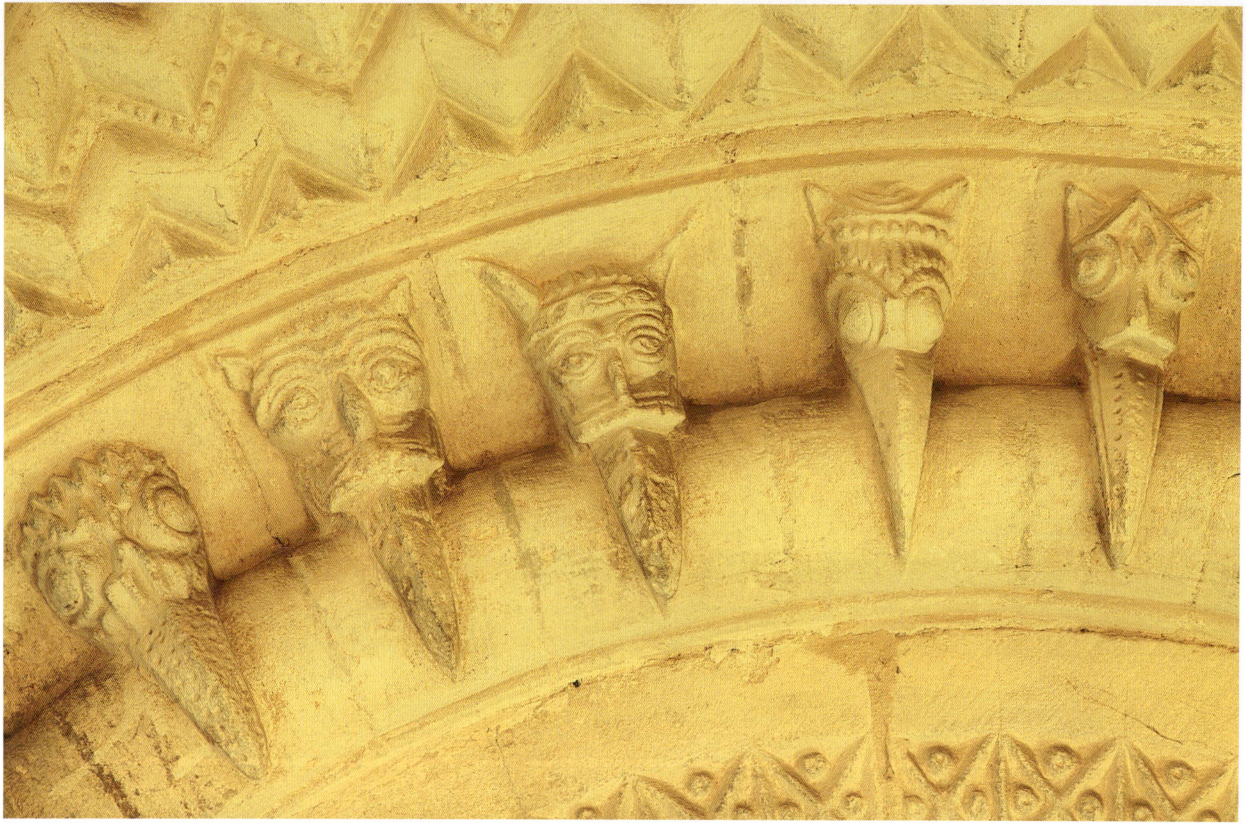

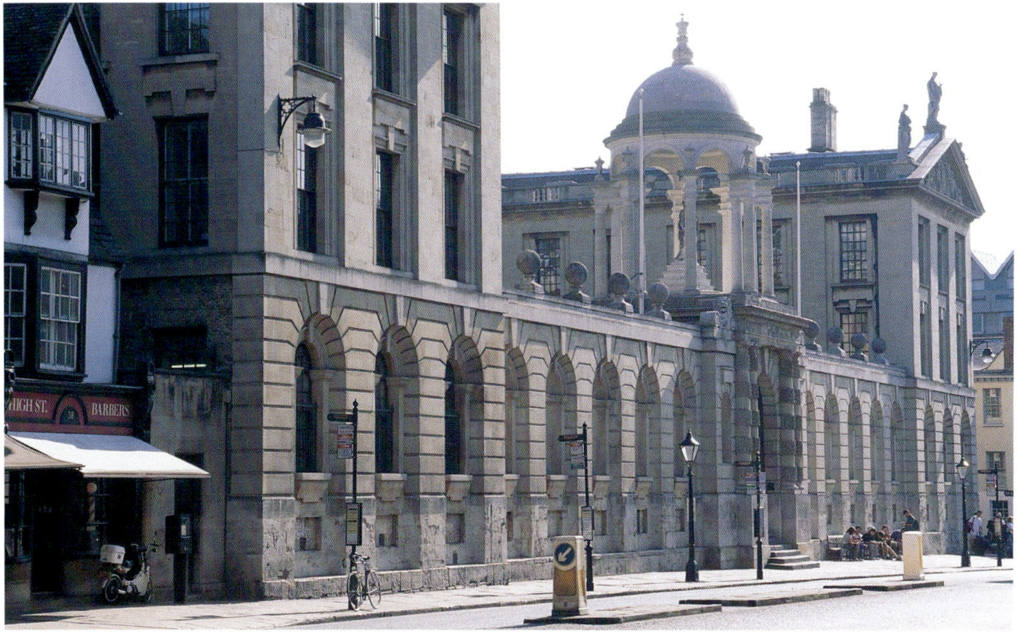

ST EDMUND HALL Library Doorway

The library of St Edmund Hall was formerly the church of St Peter-in-the-East.

QUEEN'S COLLEGE

In all Oxford there is no grander architectural statement than Queen's …

John Julius Norwich *The Architecture of Southern England* 1985

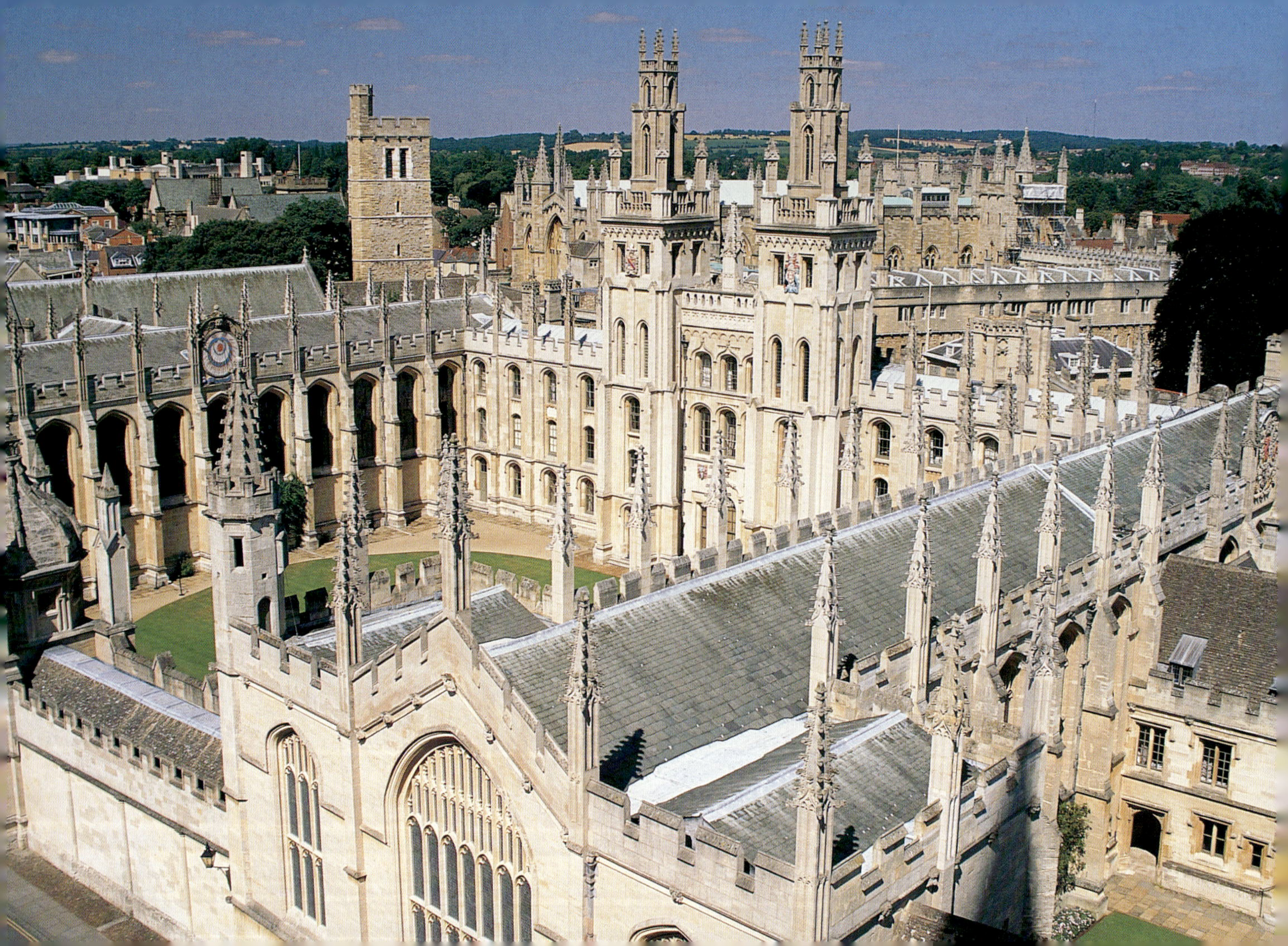

ALL SOULS COLLEGE
FROM THE TOWER OF ST MARY'S CHURCH

There is a density of monuments of architecture here which has not the like in Europe … the Oxford image is a landscape made of stone …

JENNIFER SHERWOOD AND NIKOLAUS PEVSNER
Oxfordshire (The Buildings of England)
1974

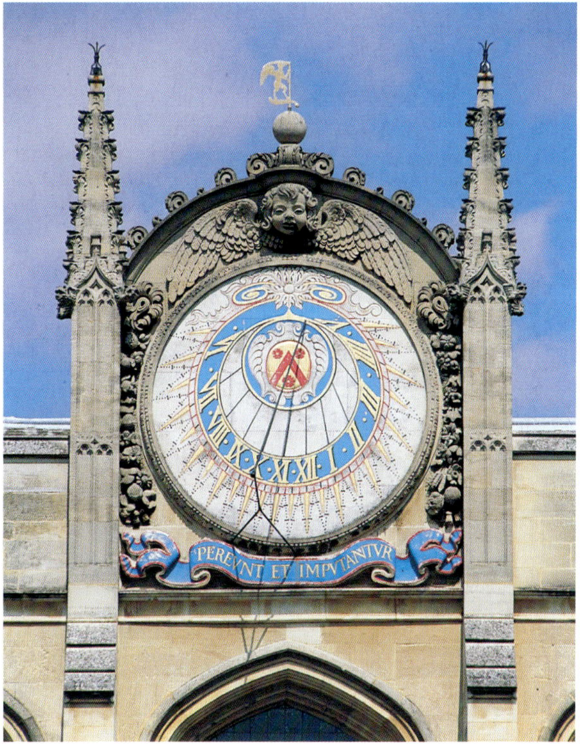

ALL SOULS COLLEGE
SUNDIAL ON THE CODRINGTON LIBRARY

… Oxford changes with every generation. It is always growing old, but it is always growing young again … By the public at large no place is supposed to be so conservative, so unchanging, nay, so stubborn in resisting new ideas, as Oxford; and yet people who knew it forty or fifty years ago, like myself, find it now so changed, that, when they look back they can hardly believe it is the same place.

F. MAX MÜLLER
My Autobiography: a Fragment
1901

BRASENOSE COLLEGE
Gateway to Radcliffe Square

... Mr Larkyns drew Verdant's attention to the brazen nose that is such a conspicuous object over the entrance-gate. 'That,' said he, 'was modelled from a cast of the Principal feature of the first Head of the college; and so the college was named Brazen-nose.'

Edward Bradley
The Adventures of Mr Verdant Green: an Oxford Freshman, by Cuthbert Bede, B.A.
1853

The fanciful stories told by amateur guides in Oxford were notoriously inaccurate!

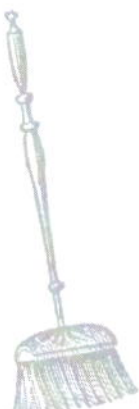

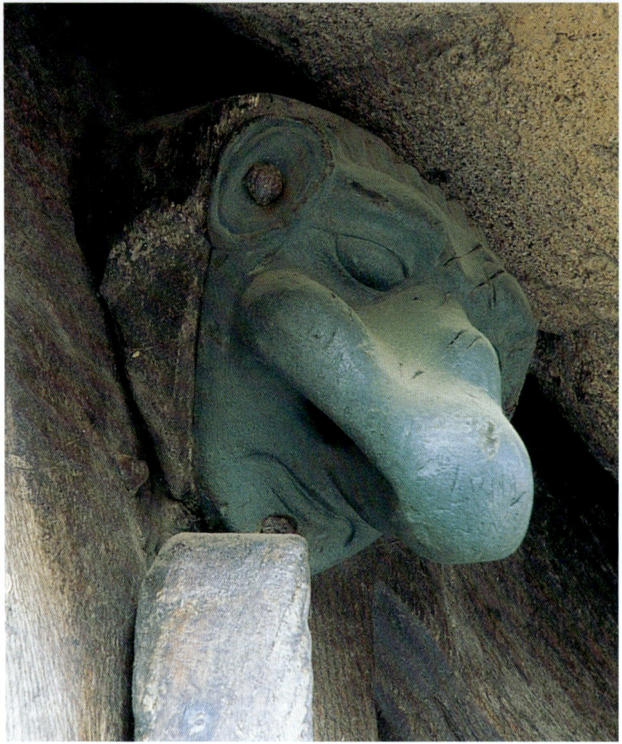

BRASENOSE COLLEGE
from Radcliffe Camera

Mr Verdant Green glanced curiously round the Quadrangle, with its picturesque irregularity of outline, its towers and turrets and battlements, its grey time-eaten walls, its rows of mullioned heavy-headed windows, and the quiet cloistered air that spoke of study and reflection ...

Edward Bradley
The Adventures of Mr Verdant Green: an Oxford Freshman, by Cuthbert Bede, B.A.
1853

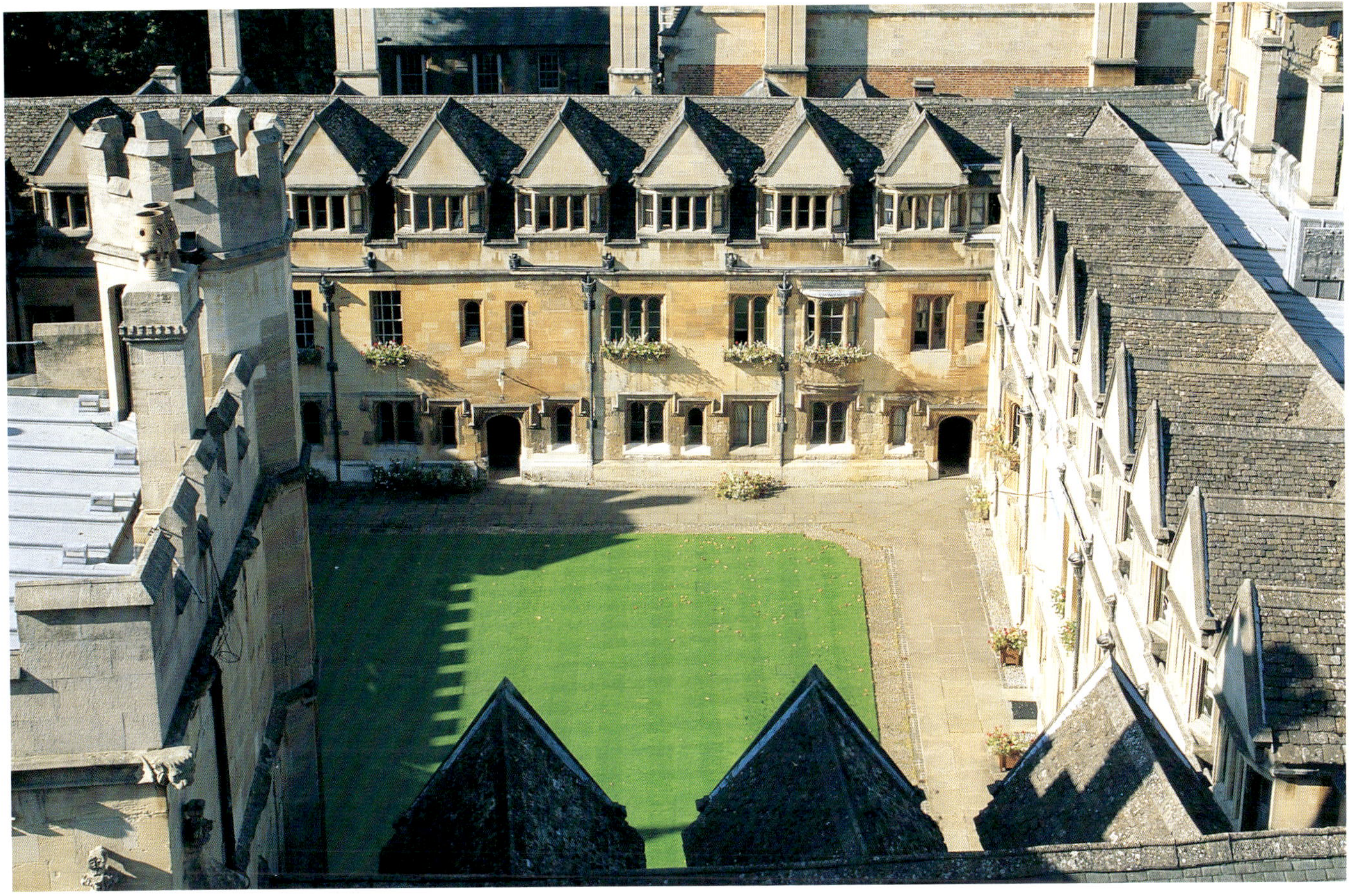

CHURCH OF ST MARY THE VIRGIN
FROM RADCLIFFE SQUARE

Queen Elizabeth I was at St Mary's listening to learned discussion for four hours on three successive days, and closing the long debate herself with a speech in Latin.

ARTHUR MEE
The King's England – Oxfordshire
1949

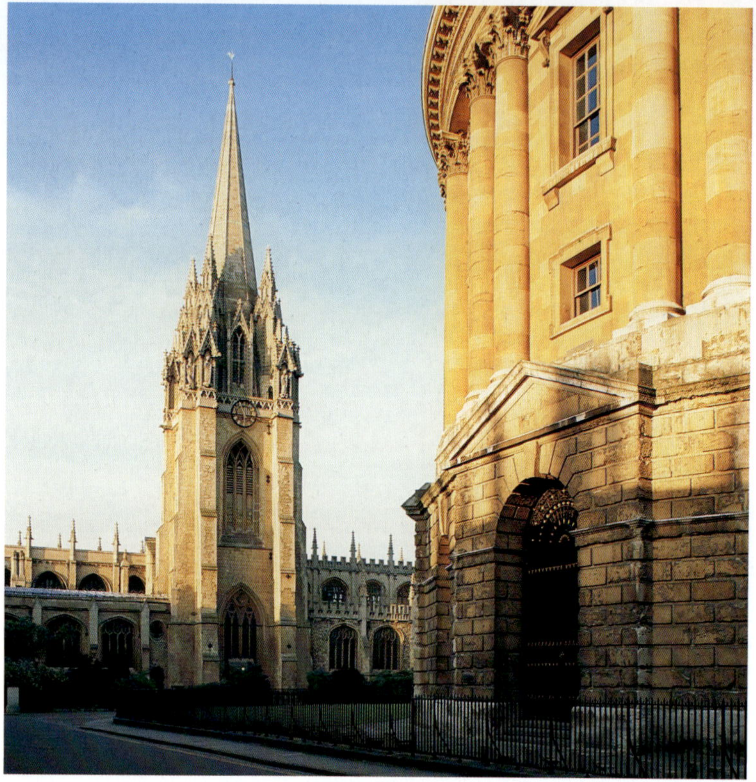

CHURCH OF ST MARY THE VIRGIN
SOUTH PORCH

The figure of the Virgin and child on this porch gave great offence to the puritans ... It was defaced by the parliamentary soldiers about five years after it was erected.

JAMES INGRAM
Memorials of Oxford
1837

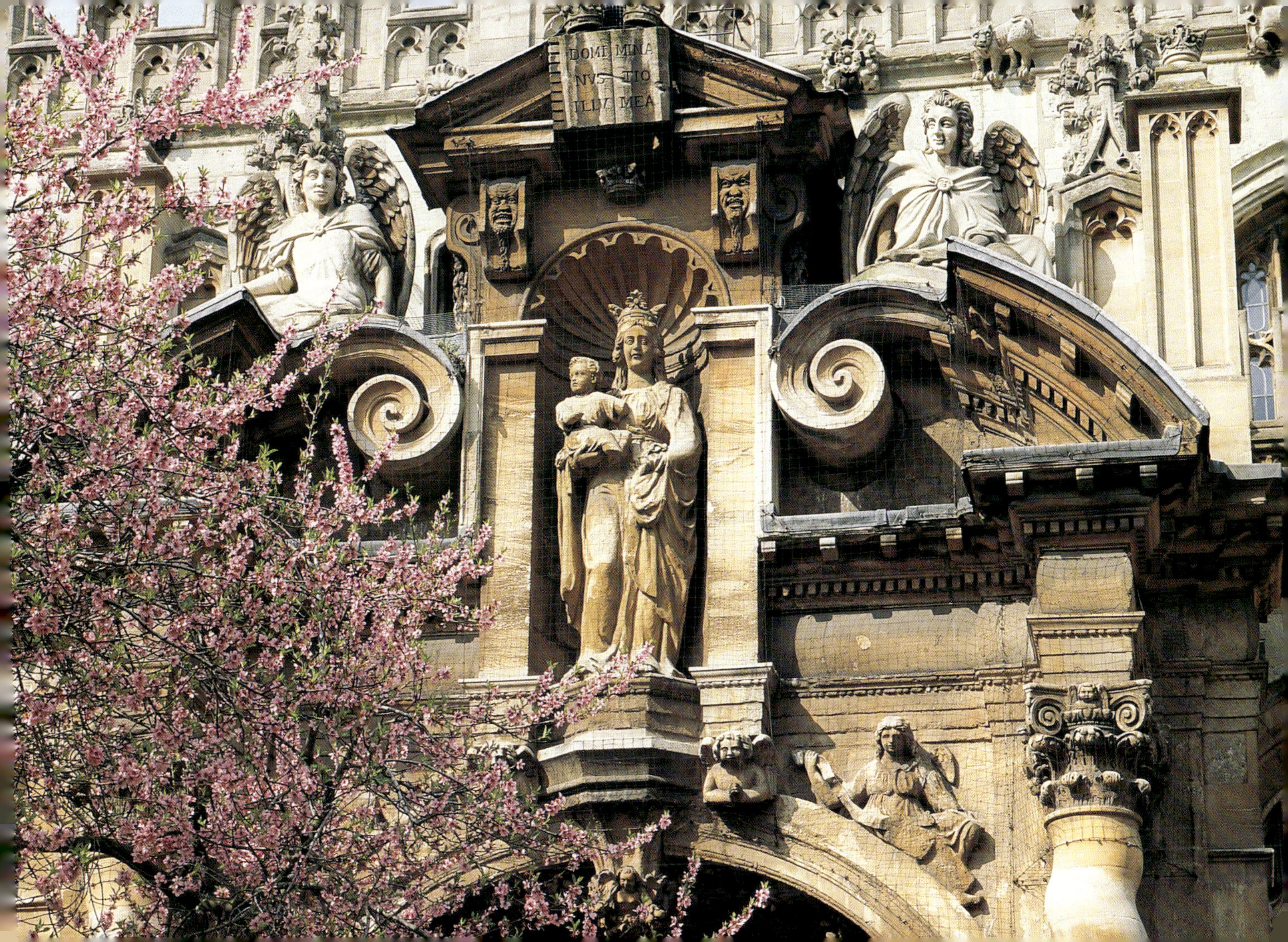
DOMI MINA
NVS TIO
ILLV MEA

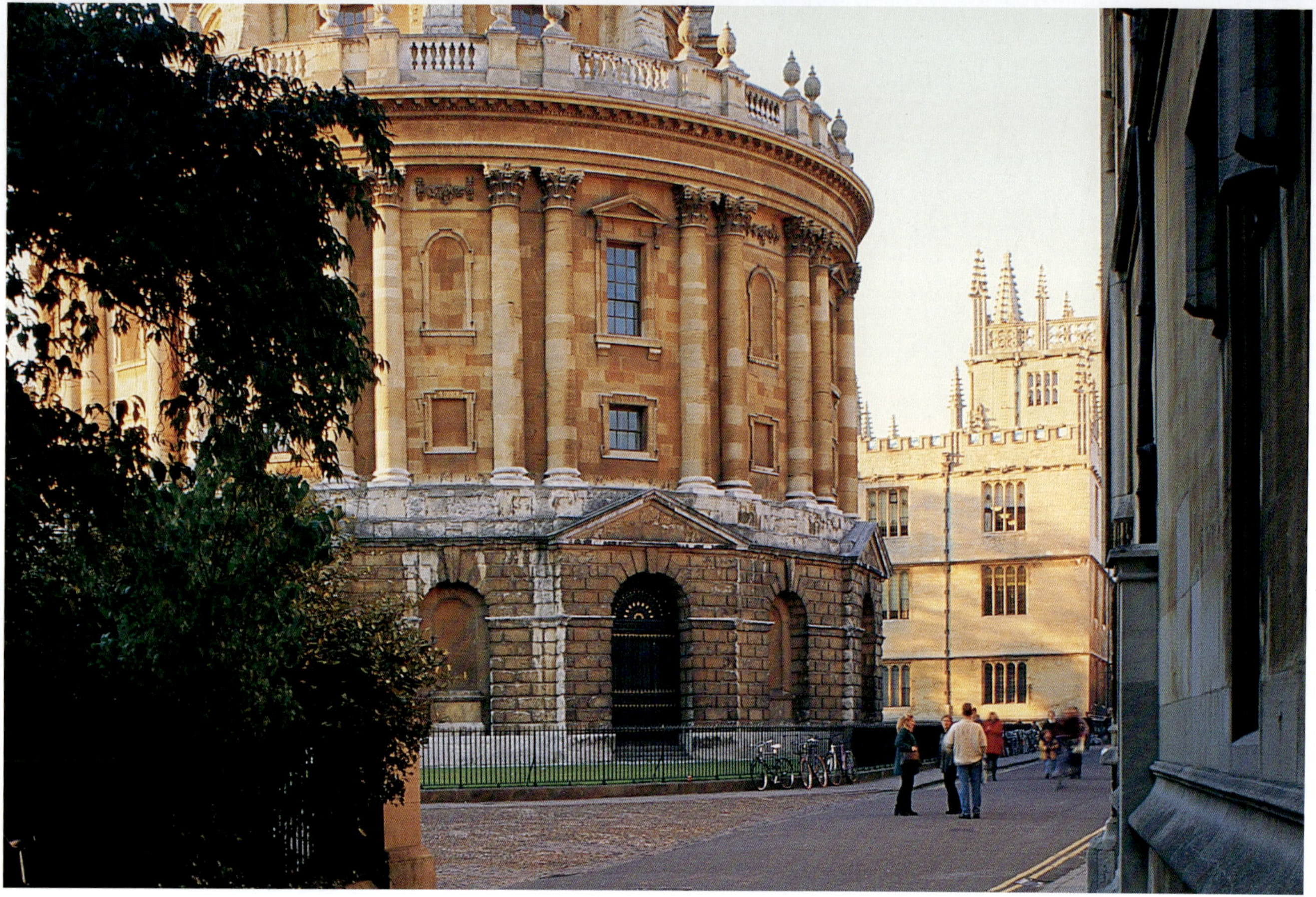

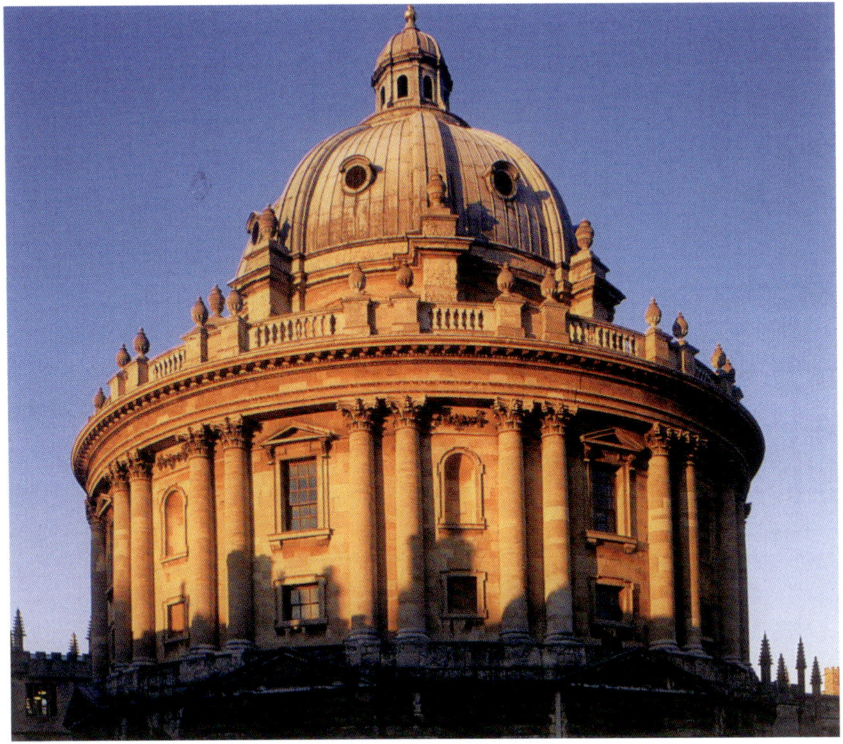

RADCLIFFE CAMERA

… in Radcliffe Square the Camera slept like a cat in the sunshine, disturbed only by the occasional visit of a slow-footed don …

Dorothy L. Sayers
Gaudy Night
1935

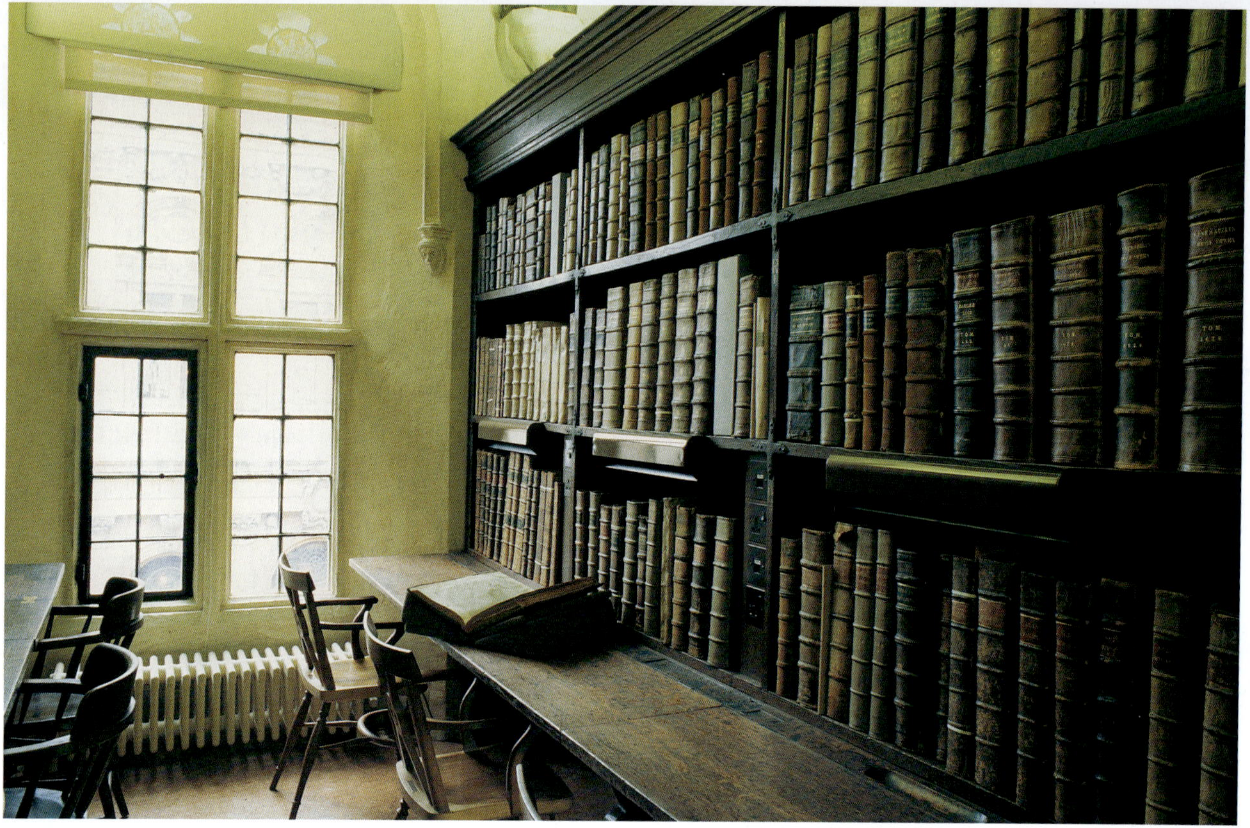

BODLEIAN LIBRARY
Duke Humfrey's Library

What a place to be in is an old library! It seems as though all the souls of all the writers, that have bequeathed their labours to these Bodleians, were reposing here … I seem to inhale learning, walking amid their foliage; and the odour of their old moth-scented coverings is fragrant as the first bloom of those sciental apples which grew amid the happy orchard.

Charles Lamb
Essays of Elia
1823

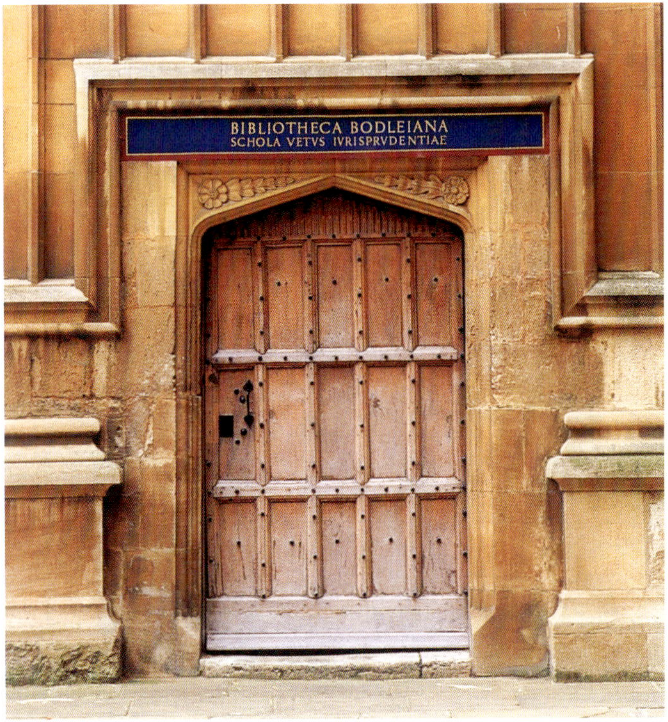

BODLEIAN LIBRARY

[Sir Thomas Bodley] who was a great student of British antiquities erected a fine library, which he furnished with many valuable manuscripts. It is still called by his name, and in consequence of the vast number of benefactions, which it has continued to receive, it is now become one of the greatest libraries in Europe.

Nathaniel Spencer
The Complete English Traveller: or a New Survey and Description of England
1773

CLARENDON BUILDING

The Clarendon printing house … exceeds, in grandeur and magnificence every structure erected for such a purpose in Europe. When the great earl of Clarendon was obliged to leave England after he had been removed from the chancery, he left his manuscript history of the rebellion, with all the profits arising from the sale of it, for building this stately structure …

N. Sanders
The Complete English Traveller
1771

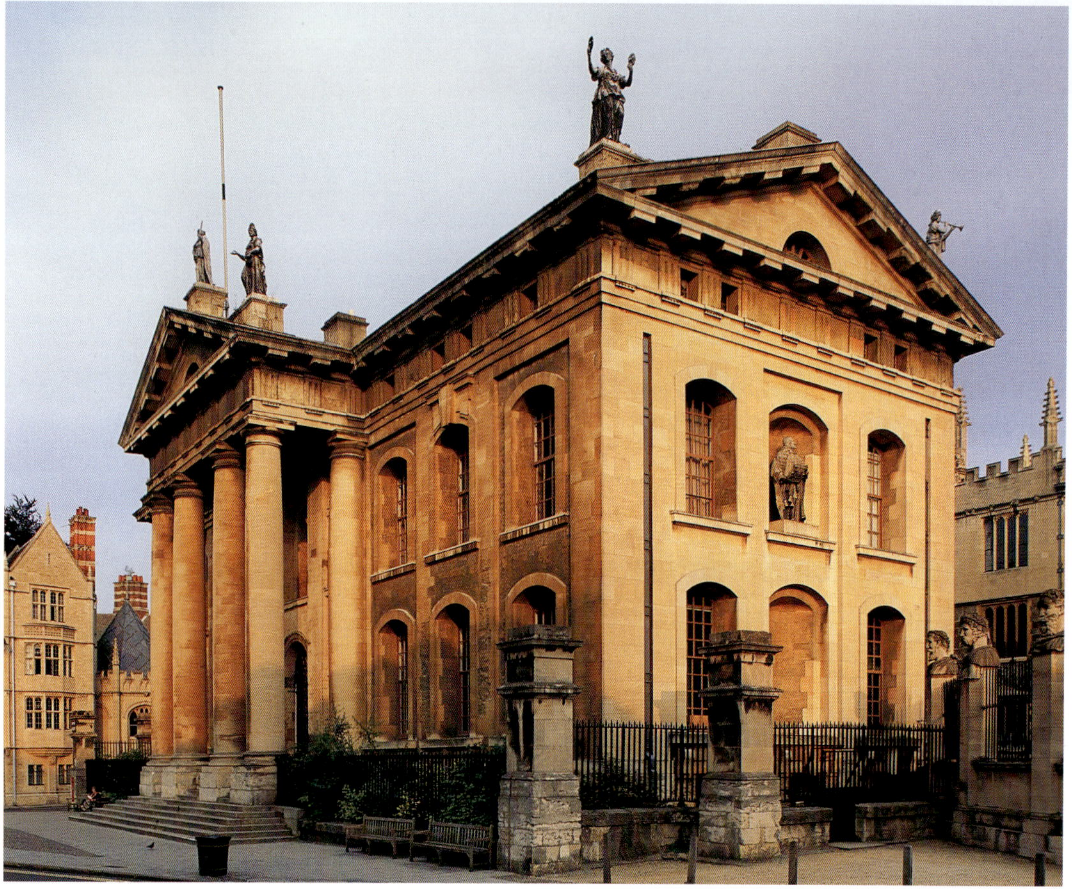

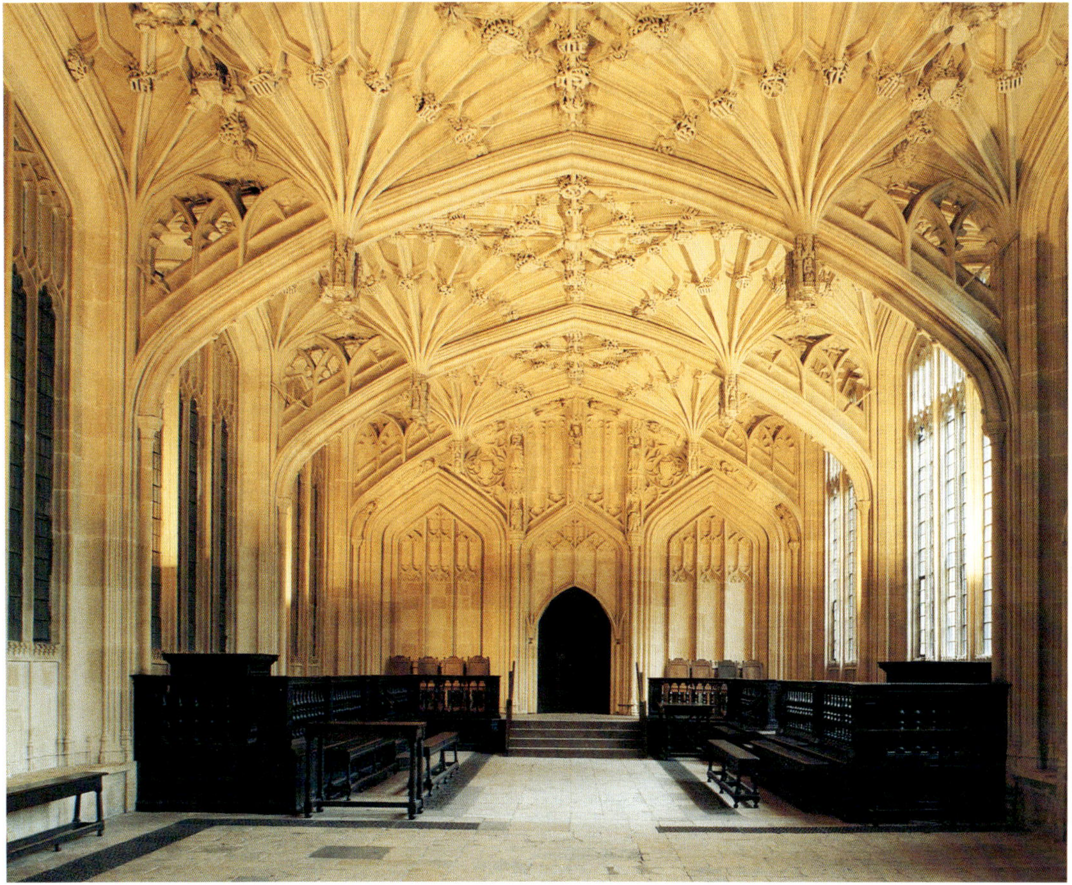

DIVINITY SCHOOL

The Divinity School of Oxford, known to tens of thousands who have attended there in cap and gown, has a vaulted ceiling of stone … They are dependent, not growing fans; and have the aspect of strengthened or reinforced umbrellas, placed upside down as would often be the case to dry off after a day and night of Oxford rain.

SACHEVERELL SITWELL
Sacheverell Sitwell's England
1986

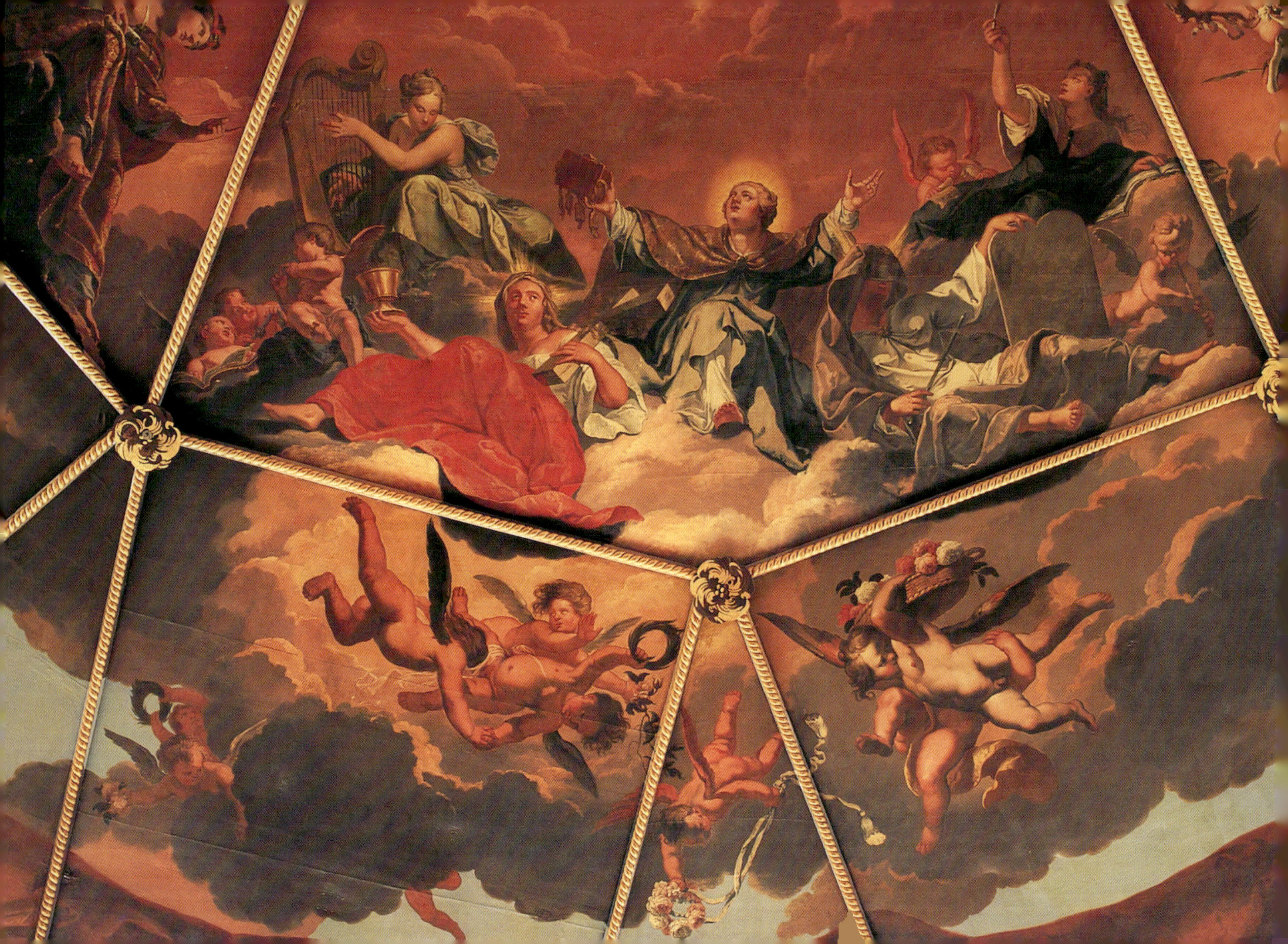

SHELDONIAN THEATRE
Ceiling

... to Mr Streeter's the famous history-painter, over the way, whom I have often heard of, but did never see him before; and there I found him, and Dr Wren, and several Virtuosos, looking upon the paintings which he is making for the new Theatre at Oxford: and indeed, they look as if they would be very fine ... they will certainly be very noble.

Samuel Pepys
Diary
1 February 1669

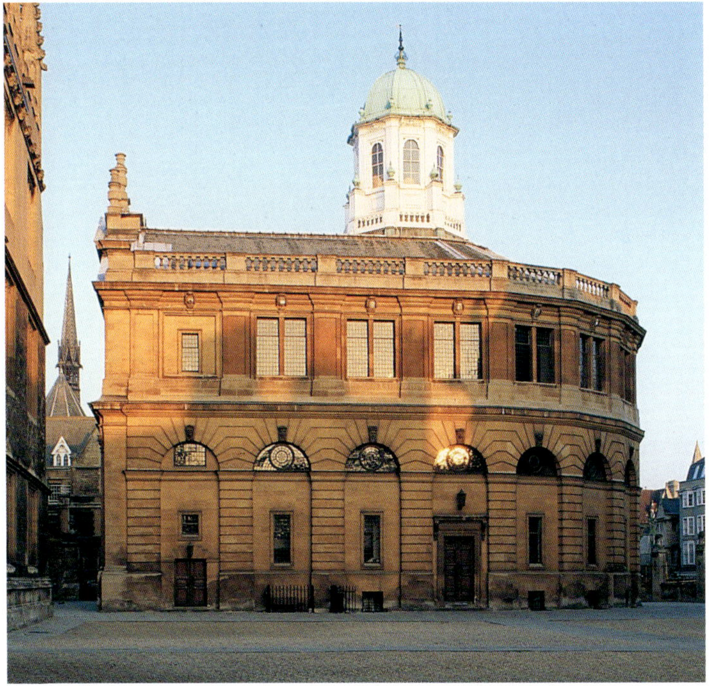

SHELDONIAN THEATRE

... there are some publick buildings which make a most glorious appearance: The first and greatest of all is the theatre ... prepared for the publick exercises of the schools, and for the operations of the learned part of the English world only, is in its grandeur and magnificence, infinitely superior to anything in the world of its kind ...

Daniel Defoe
A Tour Through the Whole Island of Great Britain
1724–26

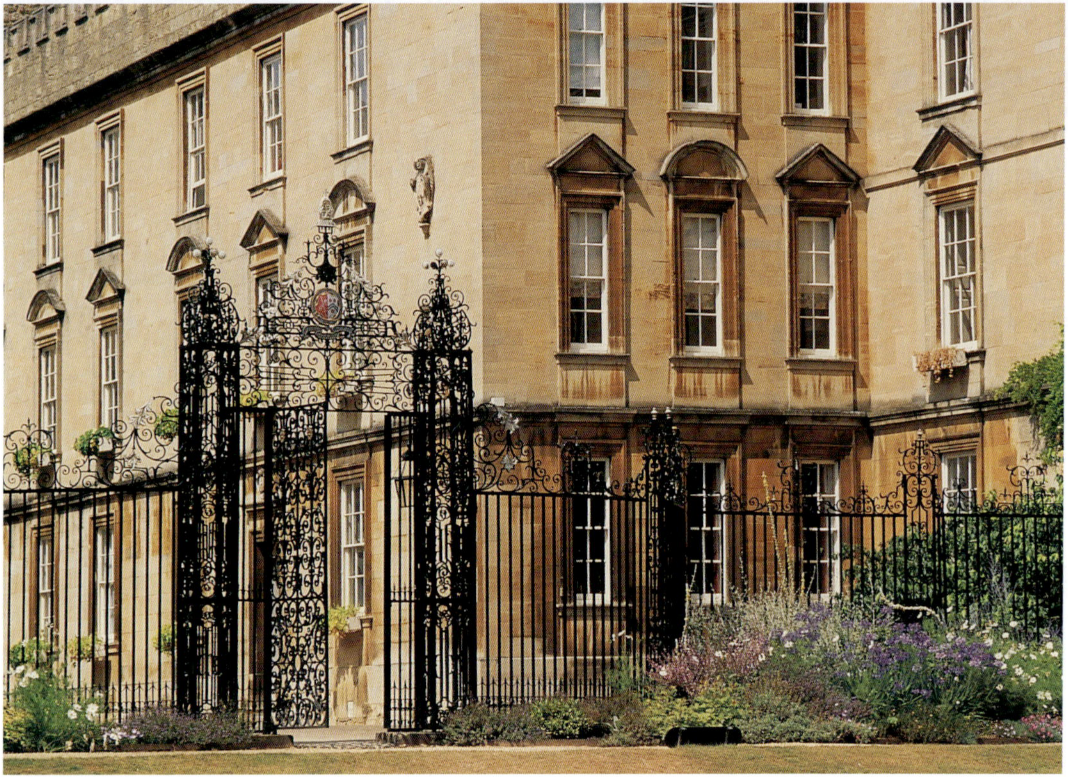

NEW COLLEGE GARDEN QUAD

Most of you … are already familiar with New College Garden, for it is *your* garden, where you can bask and give each other your private opinions … for a whole summer's day …

C. R. L. FLETCHER
A Handy Guide to Oxford specially written for the Wounded
1916

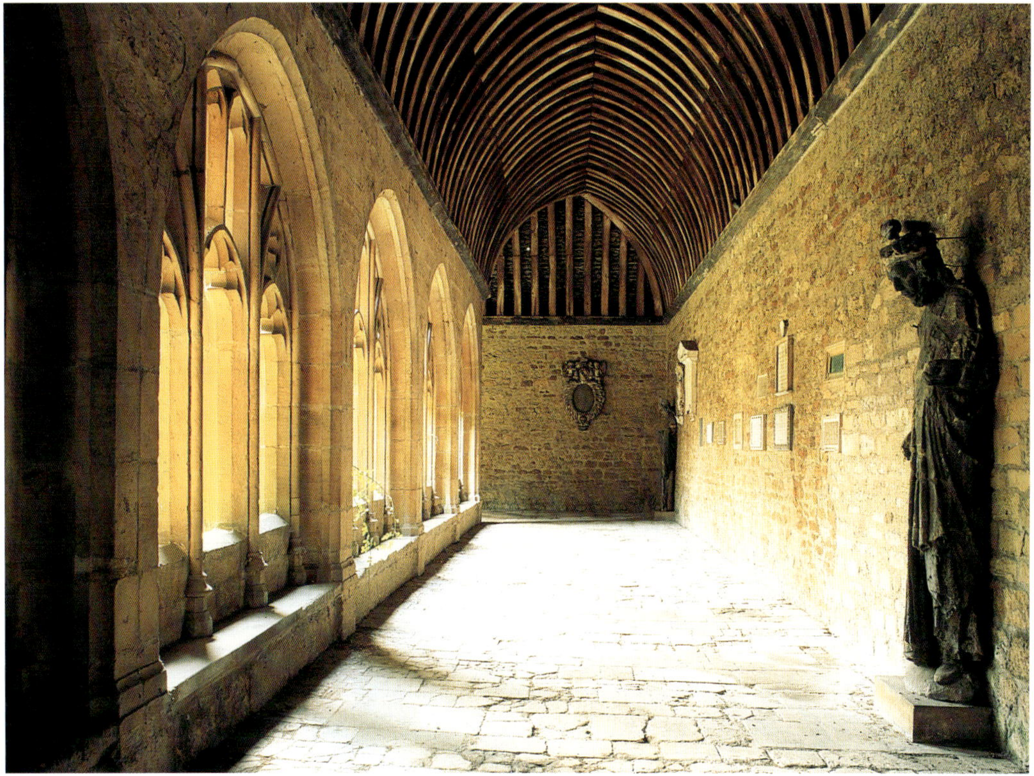

NEW COLLEGE
Cloisters

There is something about the cloisters of New College … They have an air of higher antiquity and a more severely monastic look. Indeed one half expects still to meet grey monkish figures still pacing round the stone-flagged cloisters or crossing the square open greensward in the centre and looking up and listening to the bells chiming overhead in the great grey Tower.

Francis Kilvert
Diaries
Holy Thursday 25 May, 1876

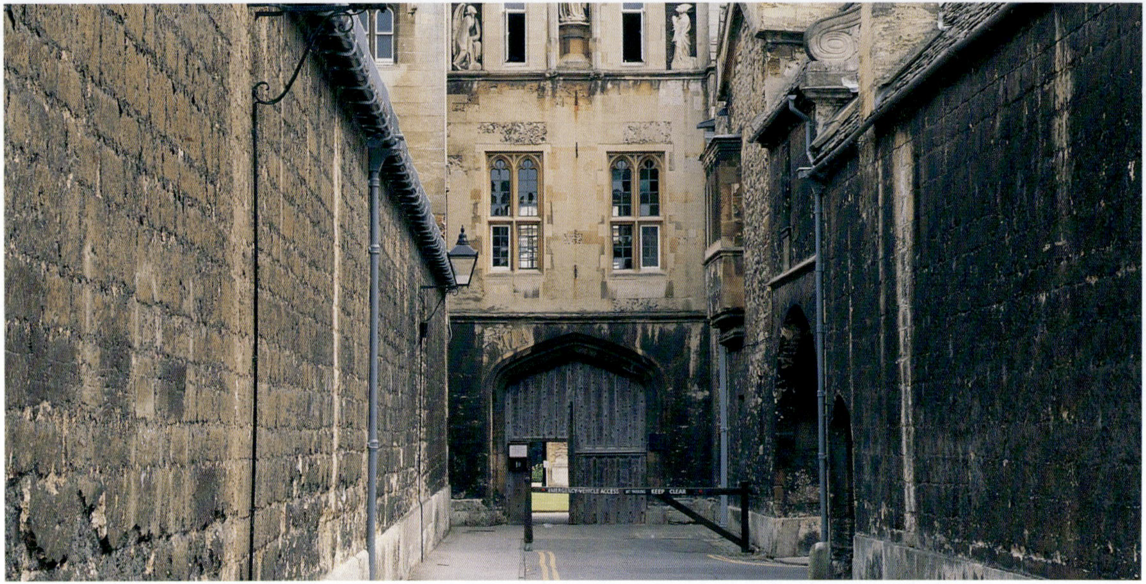

NEW COLLEGE LANE

Only a wall divided him from those happy young contemporaries of his with whom he shared a common mental life; men who had nothing to do from morning till night but to read, mark, learn, and inwardly digest. Only a wall – but what a wall!

THOMAS HARDY *Jude the Obscure* 1896

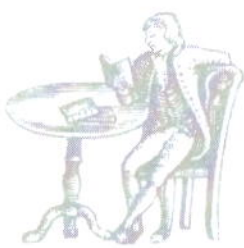

HERTFORD COLLEGE
Bridge of Sighs

It is curious that while both Oxford and Cambridge have a 'Bridge of Sighs', neither bears more than a passing resemblance to the famous bridge in Venice after which they are named.

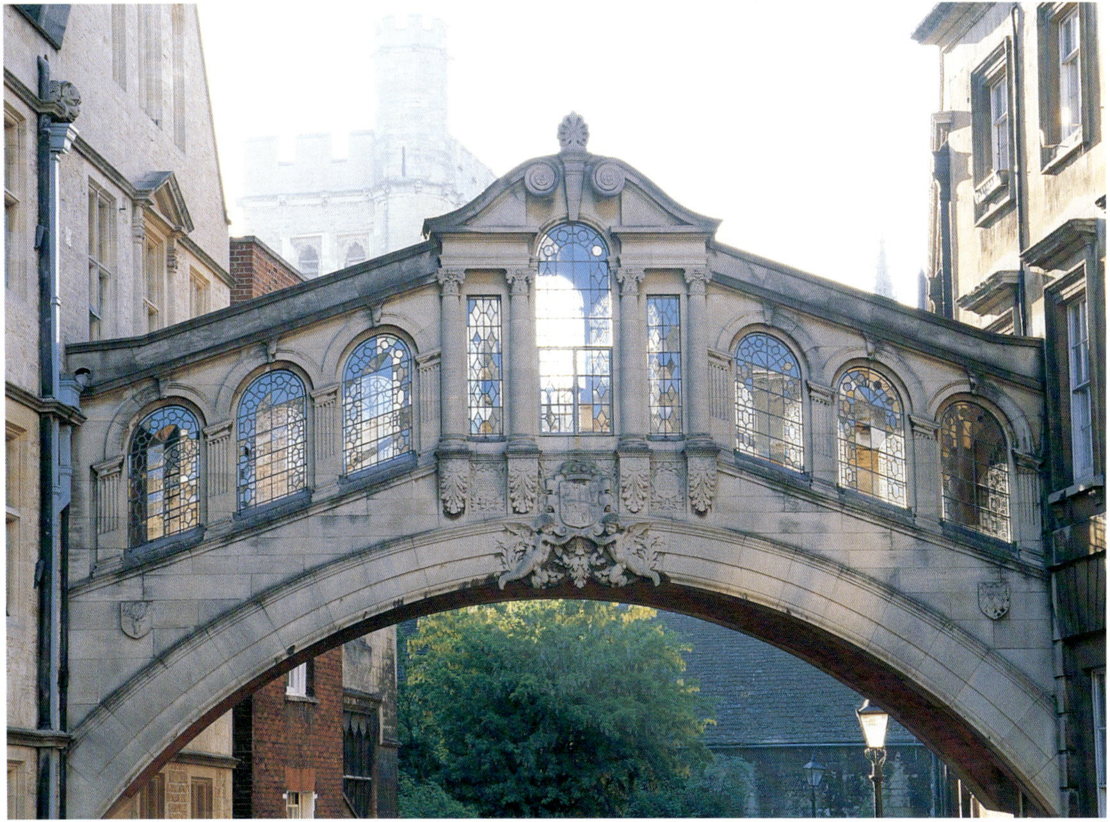

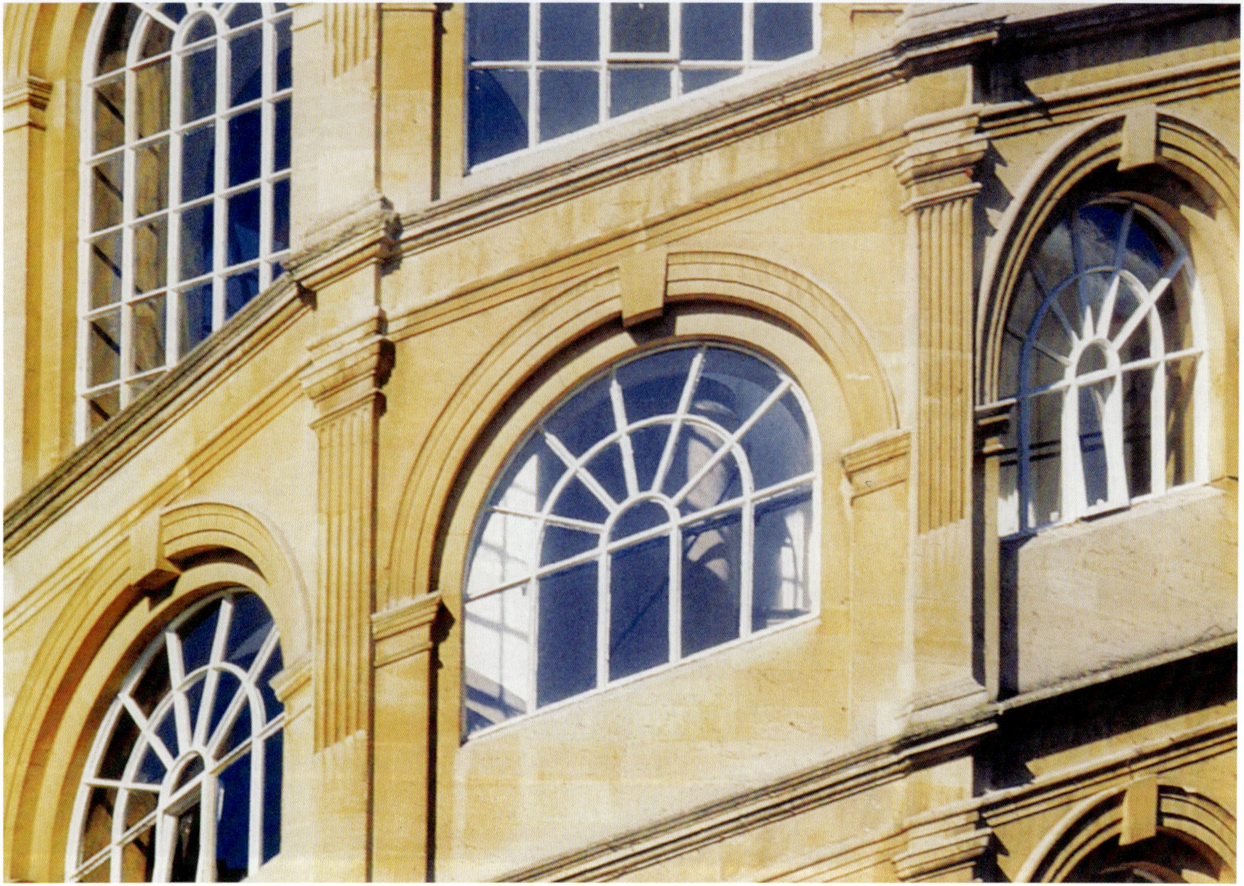

HERTFORD COLLEGE
Stair Tower in Old Buildings Quad

This college possesses the unique, if doubtful, honour of having housed the first undergraduette, or 'undie-grad' as some call them. For in about 1617 two individuals were entered at Hart Hall as gentlemen commoners, and it was not discovered for some time that one of them was a woman parading in man's clothing, so well did she play her part.

How to See Oxford
1928

Hertford College was established as an academic hall, Hart Hall, in the late 13th century. It was refounded as Hertford College in 1740.

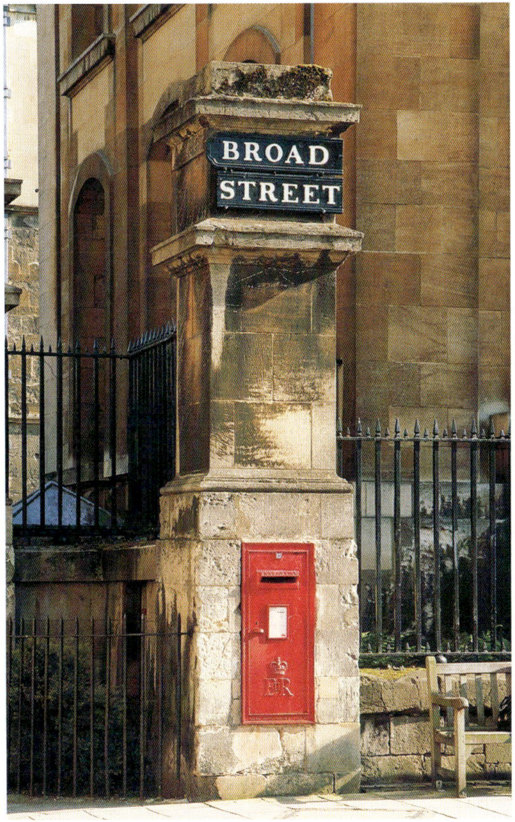

BROAD STREET

Of Oxford, with its domes and spires and minarets, its rows of shady trees, and still monastic edifices in their antique richness and intricate seclusion, I shall say nothing until I see you.

Thomas Carlyle
Letter to his brother John Carlyle
September 27
1824

HOLYWELL MUSIC ROOM
HOLYWELL STREET

... whatever were the precise reasons which led to [the Music Room] being built, it seems quite clear, from the way in which people wrote about it, that it was an unusual thing, and a thing of which those connected with it were extremely proud.

JOHN H. MEE
The Oldest Music Room in Europe
1911

Holywell Music Room opened in 1748.

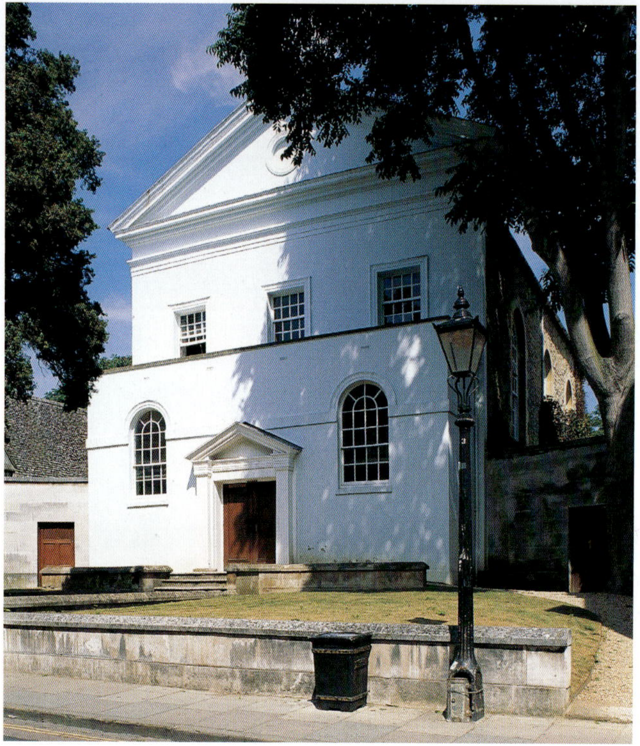

HOLYWELL STREET

... here is an effect of unfolding richness, contrast, liveliness and incident which makes Holywell Street, in its comparatively modest domestic kind, a distinguished piece of townscape in its own right.

THOMAS SHARP
Oxford Observed
1952

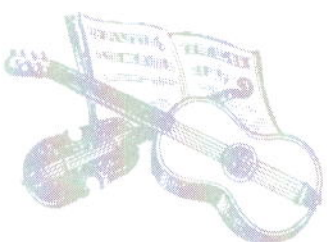

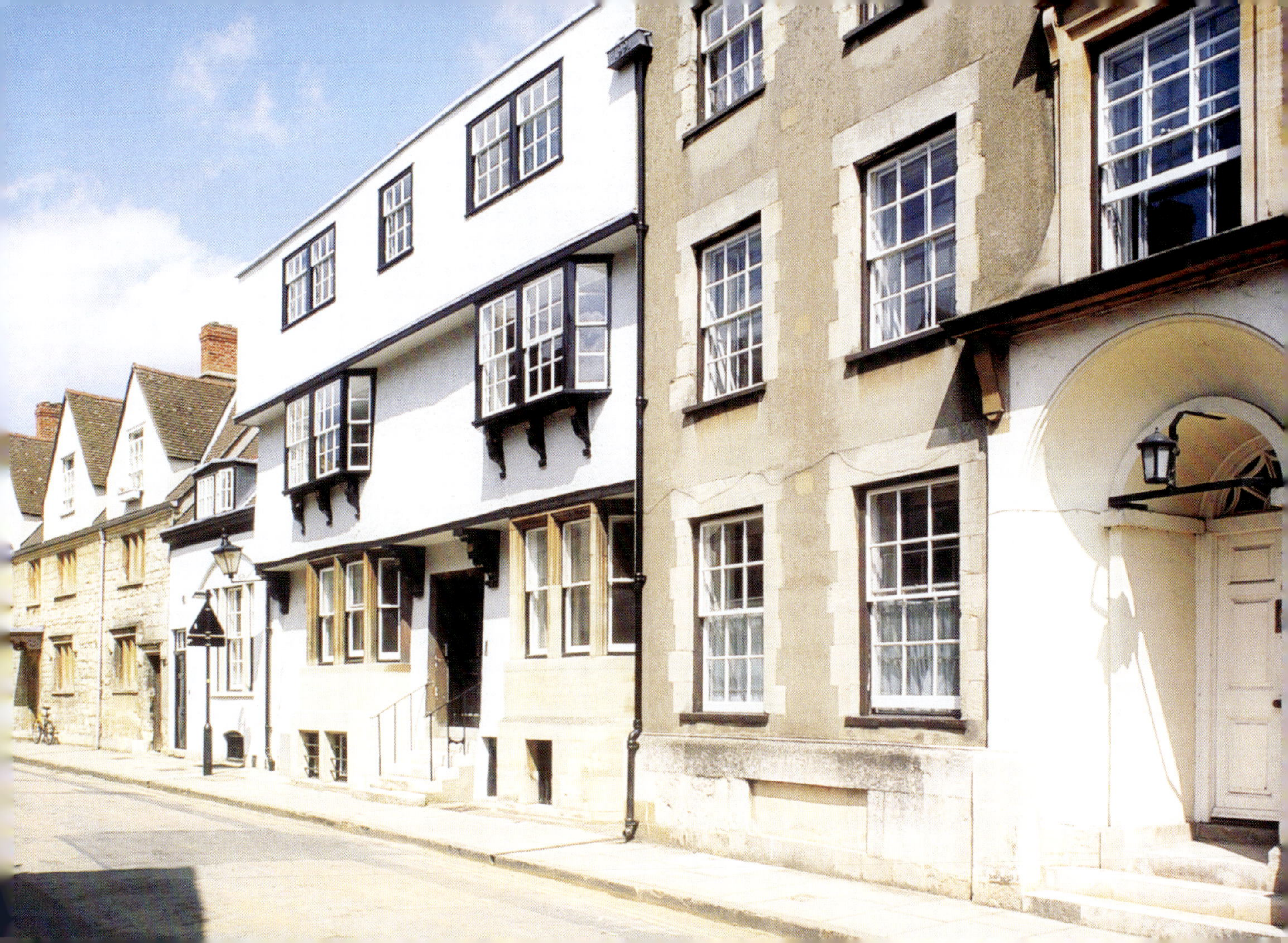

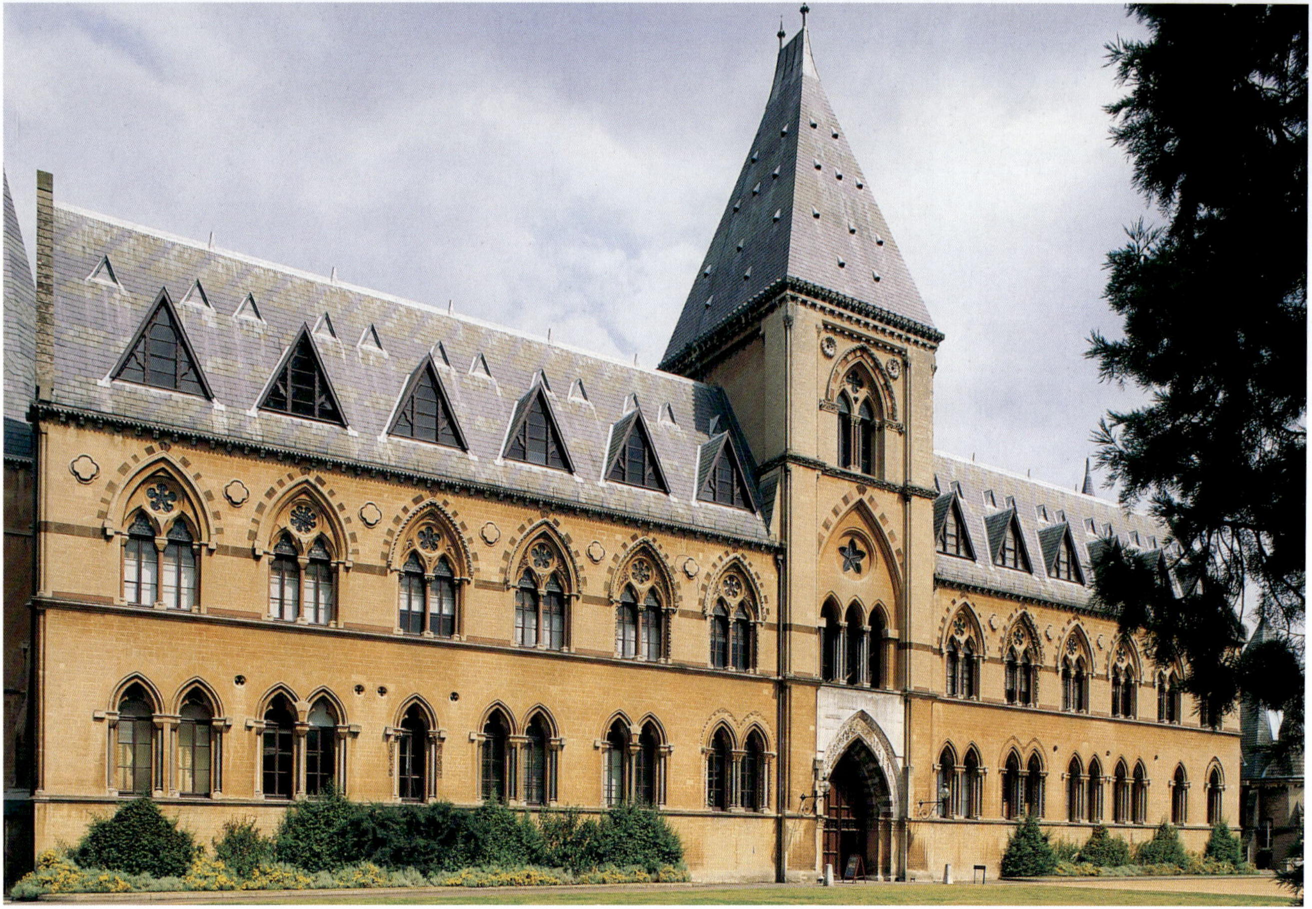

UNIVERSITY MUSEUM
Parks Road

The lovely Museum rose before us like an exhalation; its every detail, down to panels and footboards, gas-burners and door handles, an object lesson in art …

W. Tuckwell
Reminiscences of Oxford
1901

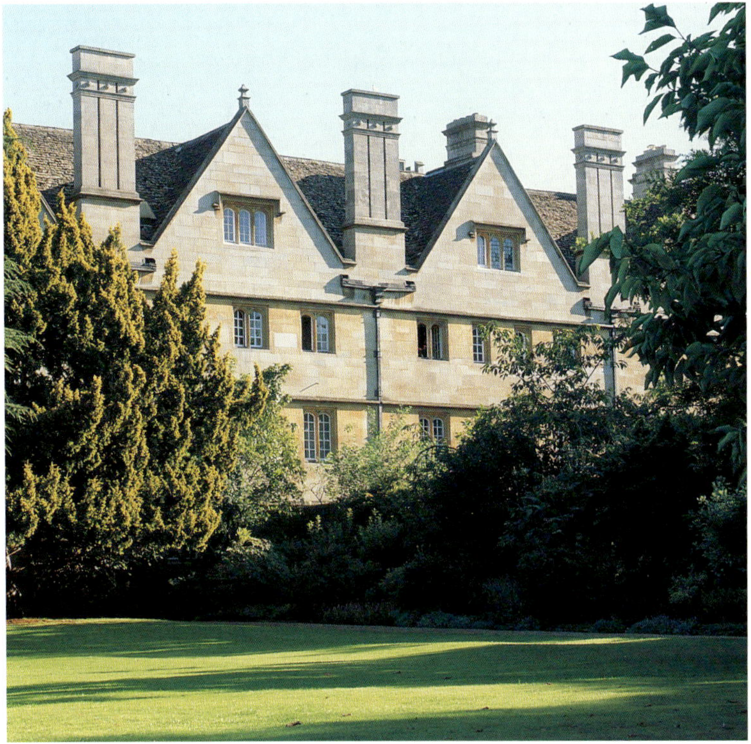

WADHAM COLLEGE
Garden

Wadham College was founded by Nicholas Wadham and his wife, Dorothy. Nicholas Wadham died before building began and it was Dorothy, then over 75 years old, who oversaw the construction of the college buildings, drew up the college statutes and engaged all the members and servants of the college. This she did from her Somerset home; she never visited Oxford and so never saw the college buildings, which were completed by 1613.

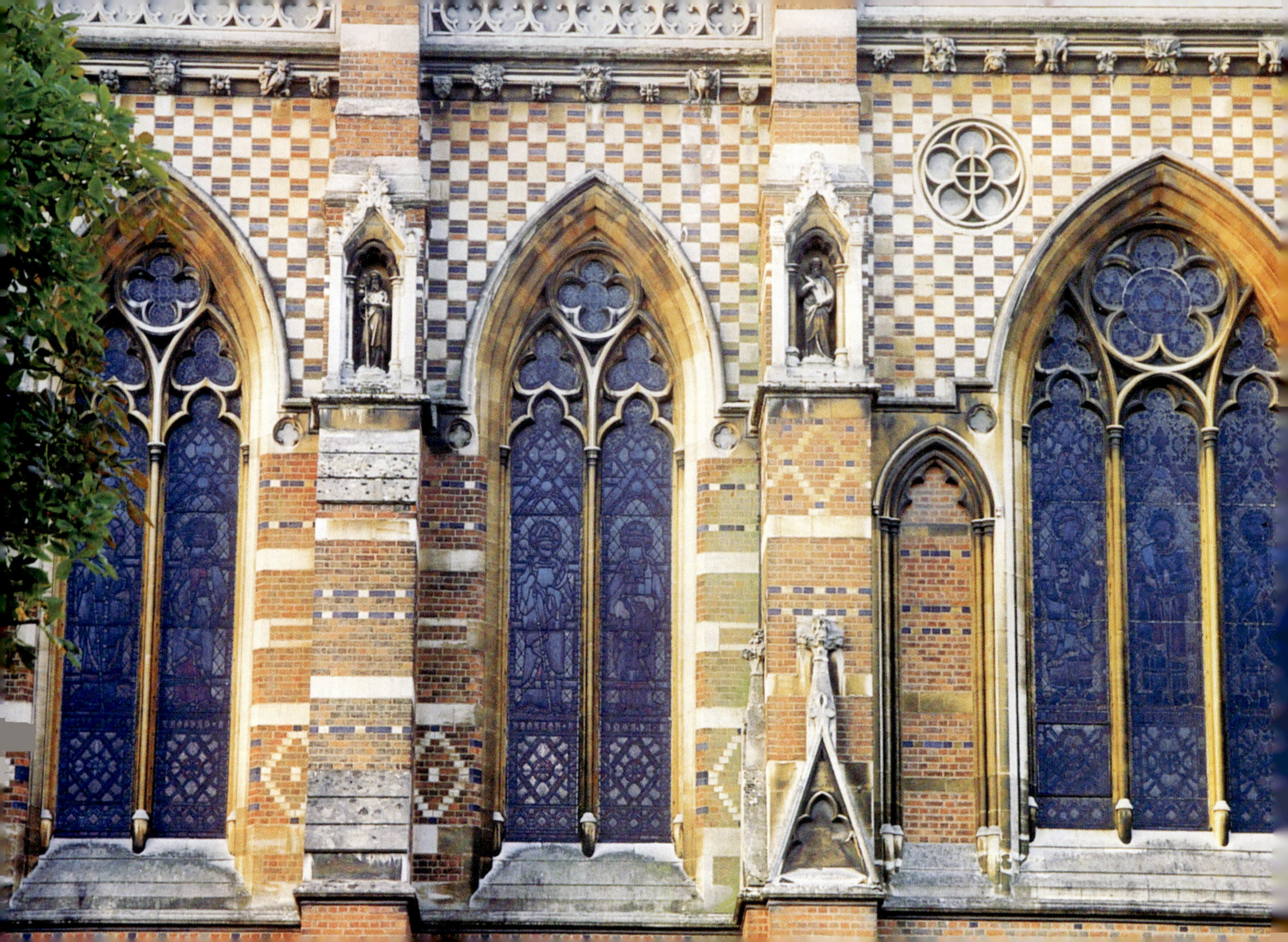

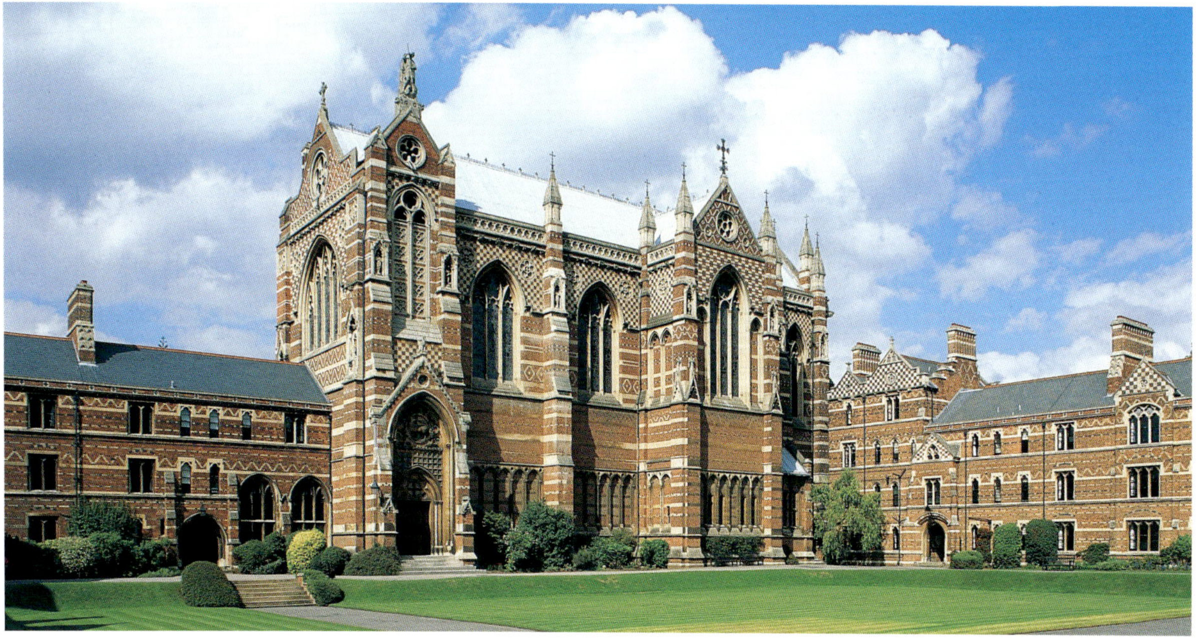

KEBLE COLLEGE CHAPEL *left*, **AND LIDDON QUAD** *above*

Among Oxford's most famous graffiti are the words said to have been chalked on the walls of Keble: 'Think not of this as a college: more as a Fair Isle sweater.'

JOHN JULIUS NORWICH *The Architecture of Southern England* 1985

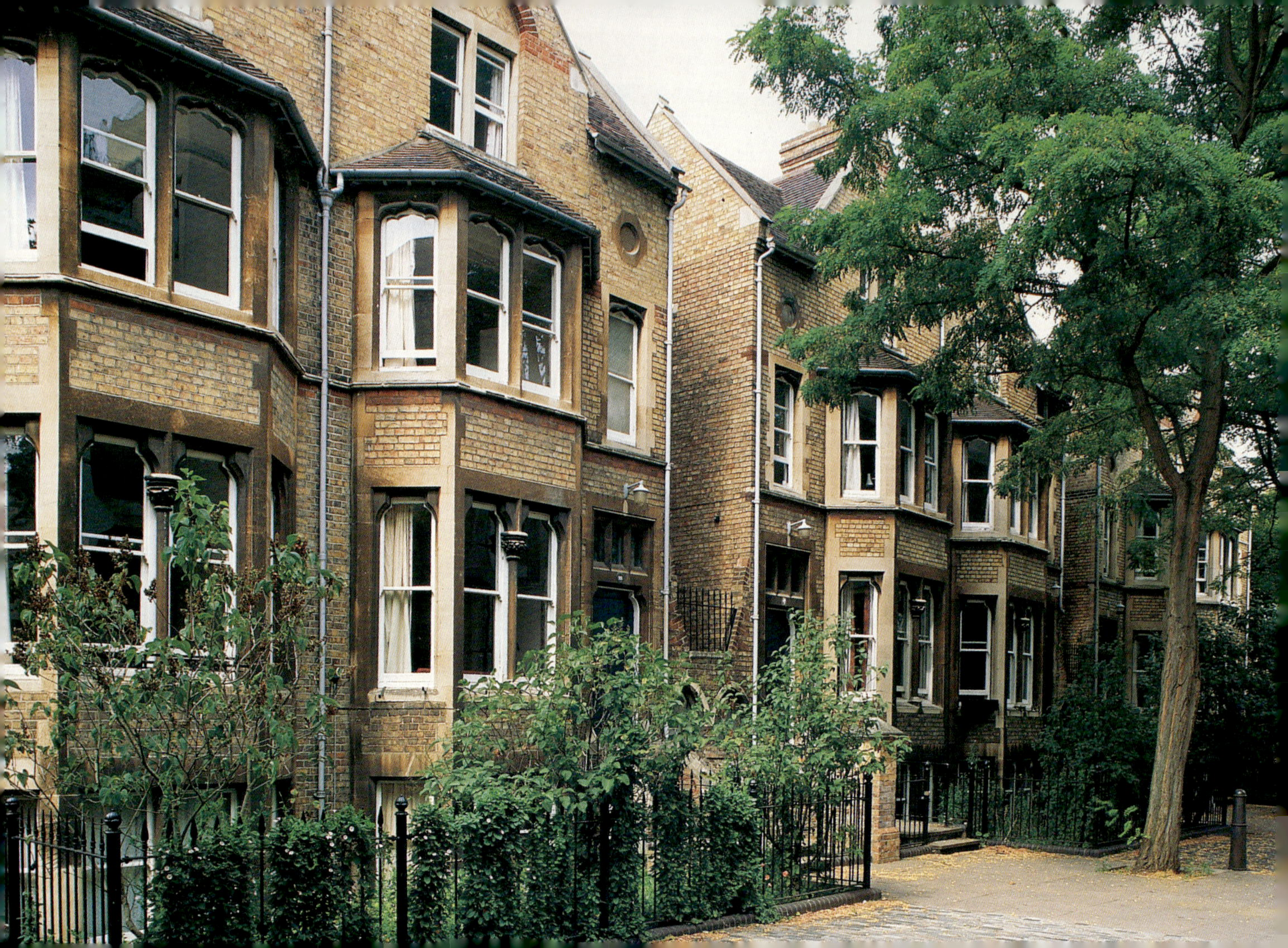

MUSEUM ROAD *left*

PARK TOWN *right*

A private trust created Oxford's first development, which, although of the mid-19th century, harks back to the gracious 18th-century crescents of Cheltenham. The Park Town estate was a 'tontine', that is, a speculation in which the investing partners agree that the last to survive will inherit the whole of the assets.

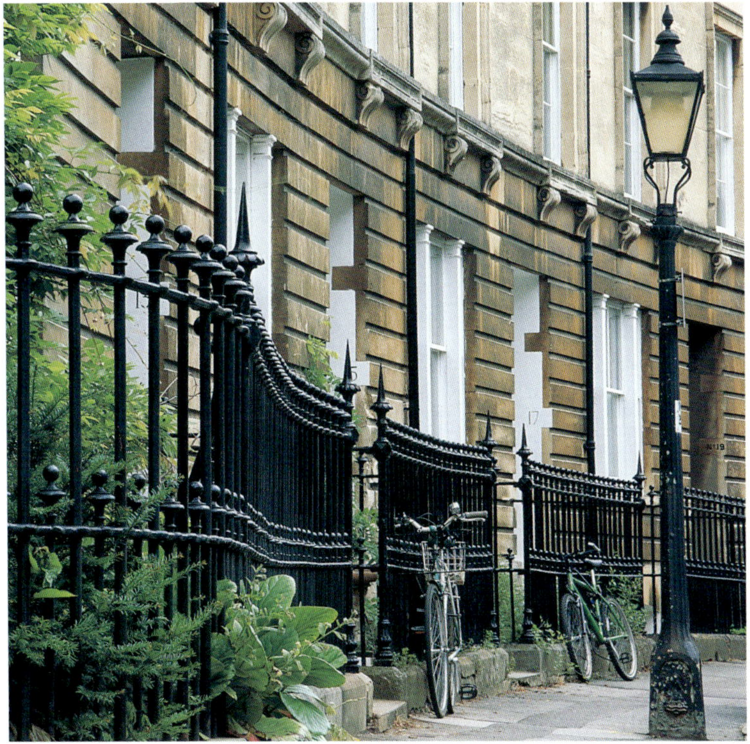

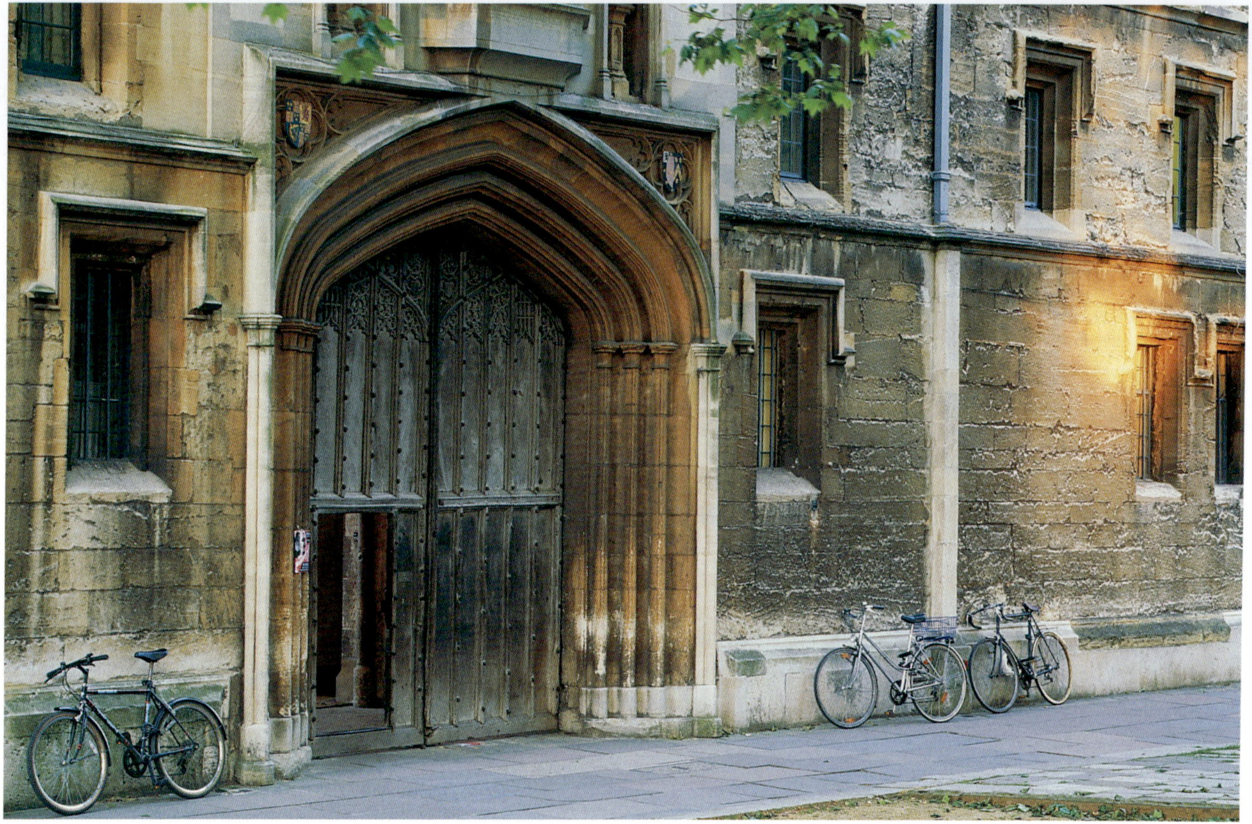

ST JOHN'S COLLEGE

What is an Oxford College like? It is, in the first place, not quite like any other Oxford College, because each has its own history and customs.

J. H. B. Peel
Peel's England
1977

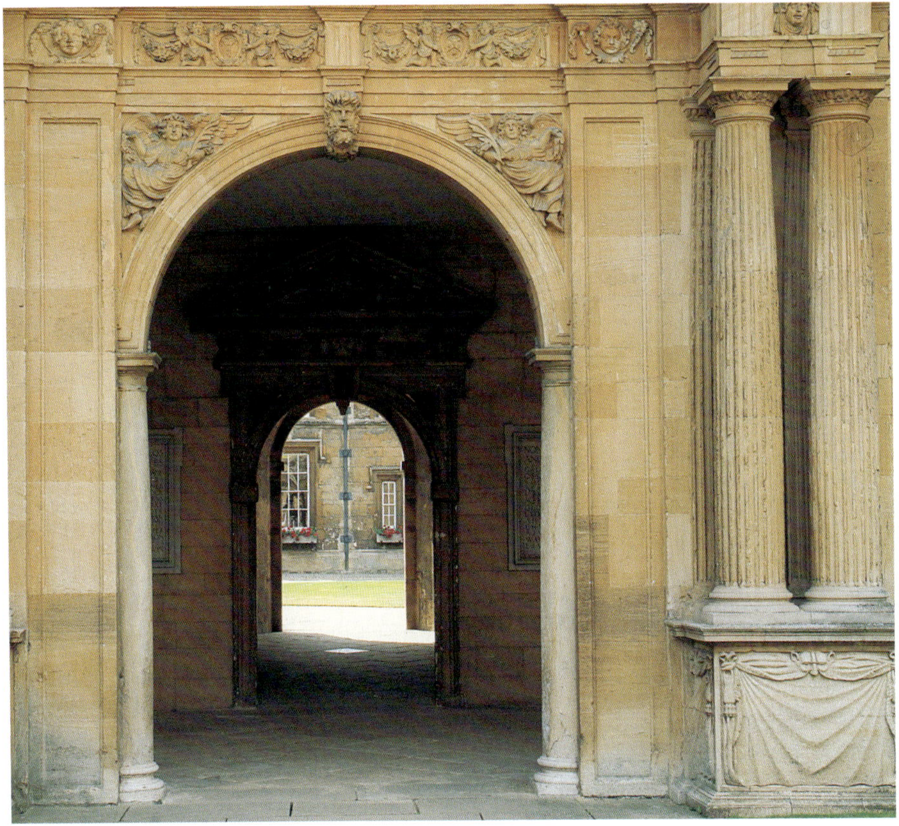

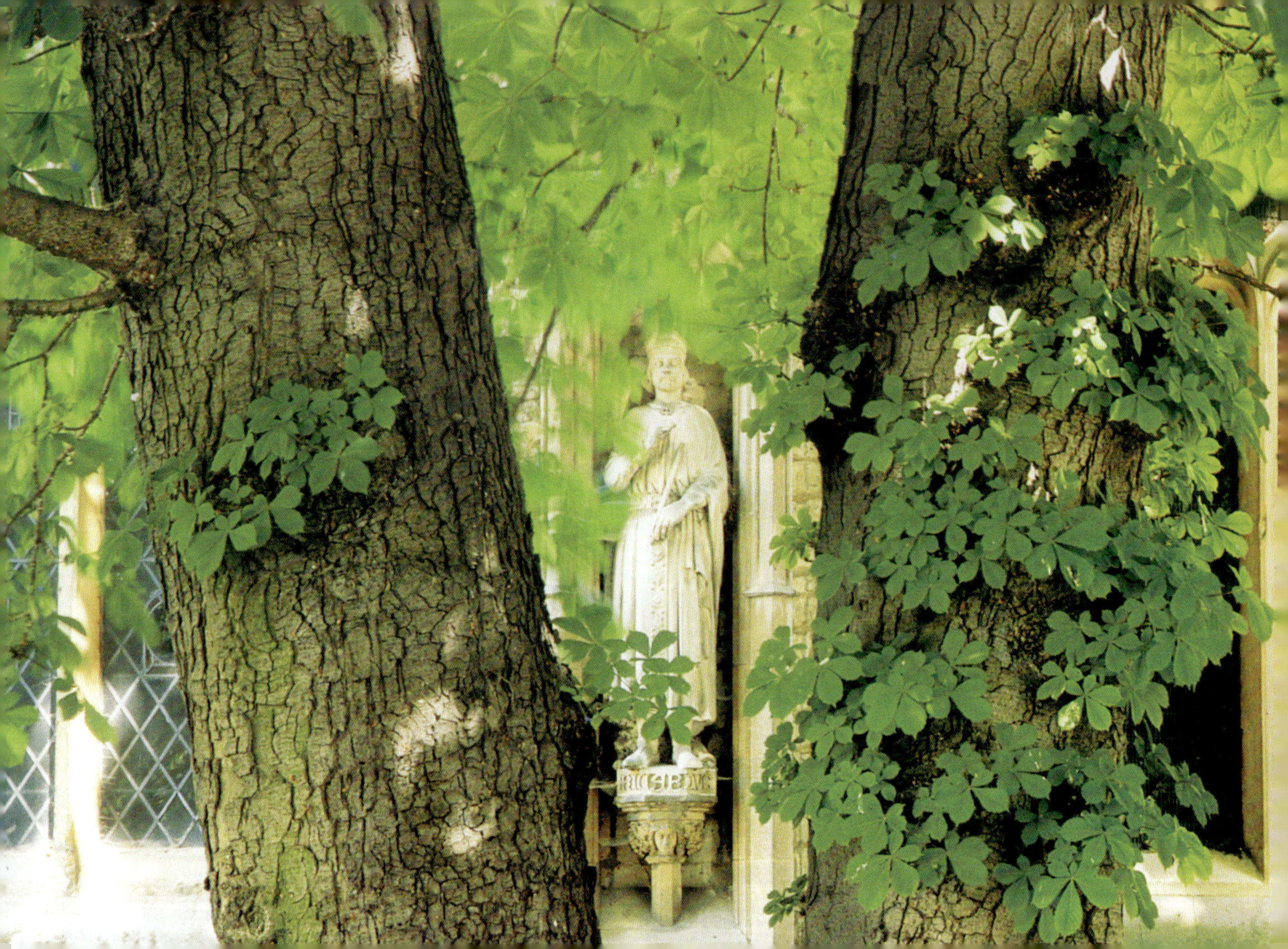

CHURCH OF ST MARY MAGDALEN
St Giles

Look up almost anywhere in the city centre and there a statue will be looking down on the busy streets.

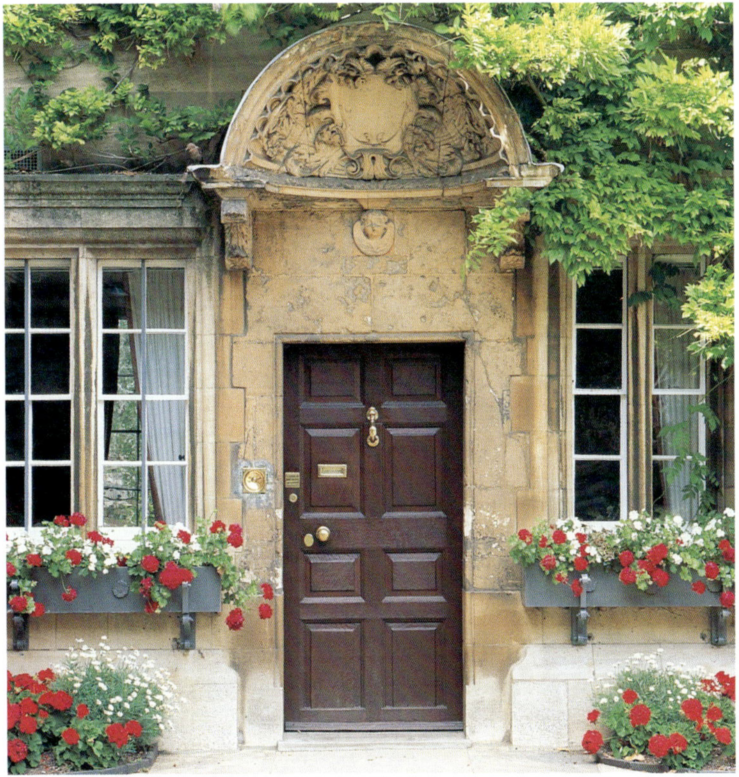

JESUS COLLEGE
Front Quad

Jesus is the famous Welsh college … they say that if you had put your head inside the first quad and called out 'Jones' a dozen heads would have appeared from as many different windows.

C. R. L. Fletcher
A Handy Guide to Oxford specially written for the Wounded
1916

MARTYRS' CROSS
Broad Street

The group progressed to Broad Street, where Downes brought them all to a stop again, this time immediately outside the Master's Lodge at Balliol. 'Here – on your left here – the plaque on the wall – this is where Latimer and Ridley, and later Cranmer, were burned at the stake ... You can see the actual spot, the cross there ... right in the middle of the road.'

Colin Dexter
The Jewel that was Ours
1991

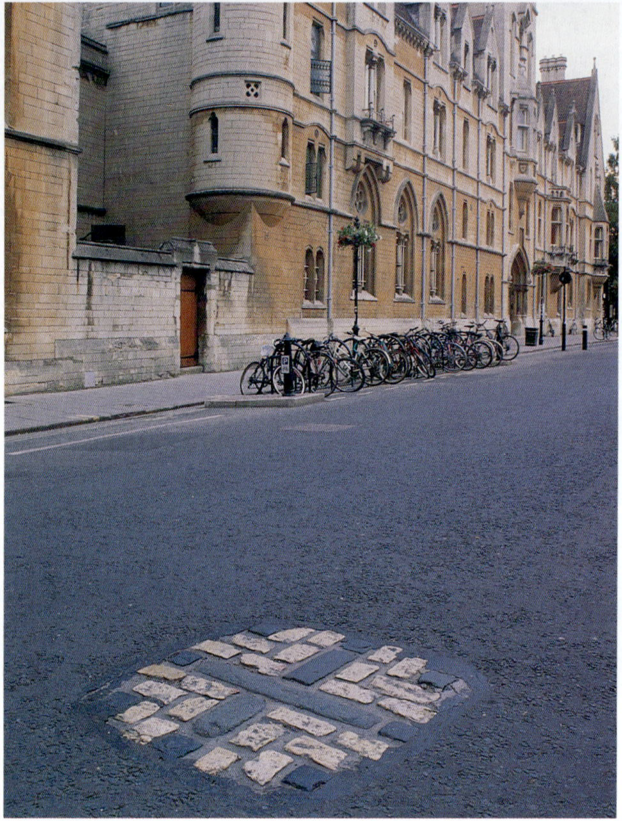

BALLIOL COLLEGE
Front Quad

'What is the essential Balliol?' Michael demanded. 'Who could say so easily? Perhaps it's the same sort of spirit, slightly filtered down through modern conditions, as you found in Elizabethan England.'

Compton Mackenzie
Sinister Street
1913

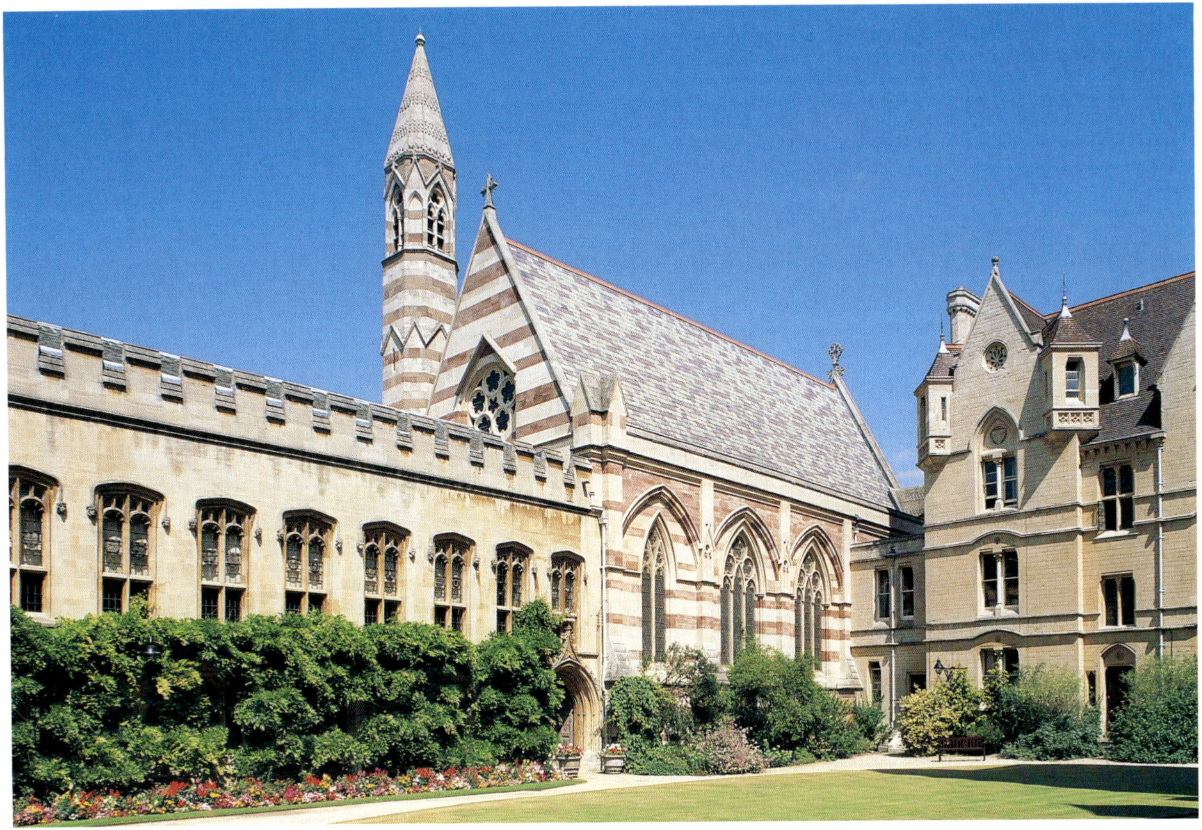

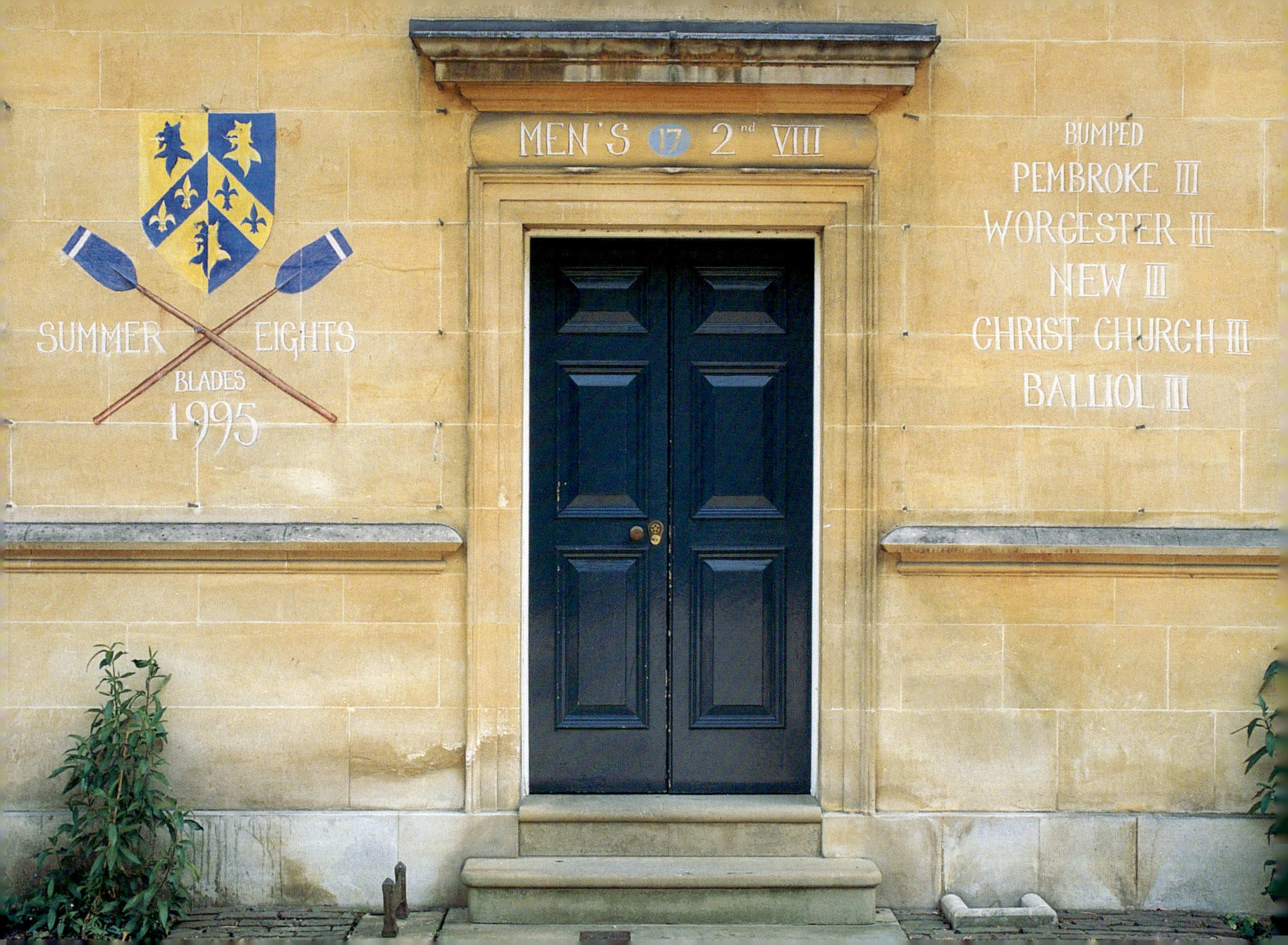
MEN'S 17 2nd VIII
SUMMER EIGHTS
BLADES
1995
BUMPED
PEMBROKE III
WORCESTER III
NEW III
CHRIST CHURCH III
BALLIOL III

TRINITY COLLEGE
Garden Quad

Colleges' rowing achievements are proudly displayed around doorways and windows – a colourful Oxford tradition.

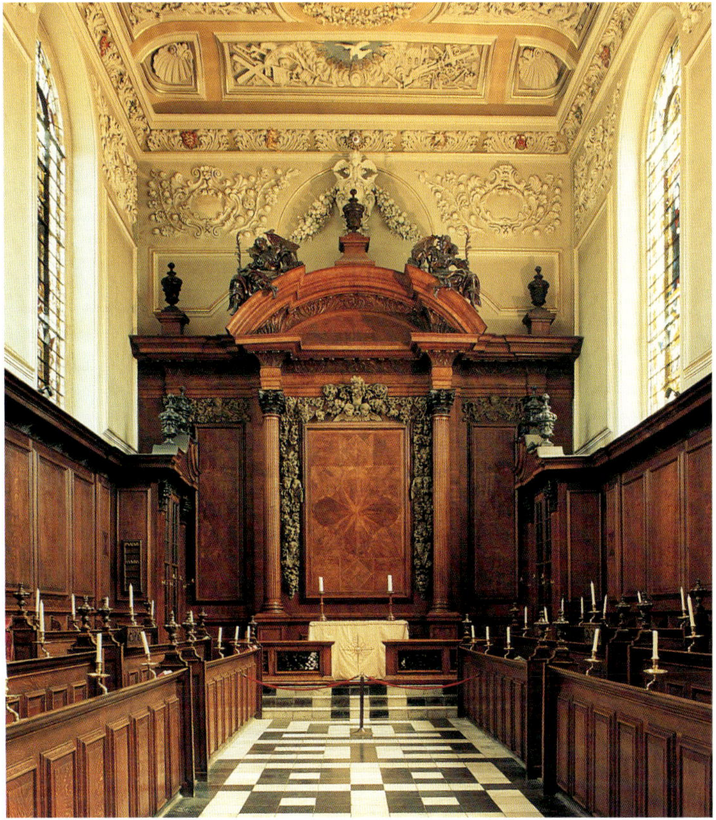

TRINITY COLLEGE
Chapel

Trinity Colledge Chapple … now is a beautifull magnifficent Structure, its lofty and curiously painted the roofe and sides the history of Christ's ascention and very fine Carving of thin white wood just like that at Windsor …

Celia Fiennes
The Journeys of Celia Fiennes
*c.*1694

TURL STREET

The view all the way down Turl Street … with the narrow-spaced buildings framing the tower and spire of All Saints as it steps out into the middle of the street and forces the roadway to take a sudden narrow twist, could hardly be more ingeniously contrived if it had been designed by a 'Renaissance' planner for a most deliberate spectacular effect.

Thomas Sharp
Oxford Observed
1952

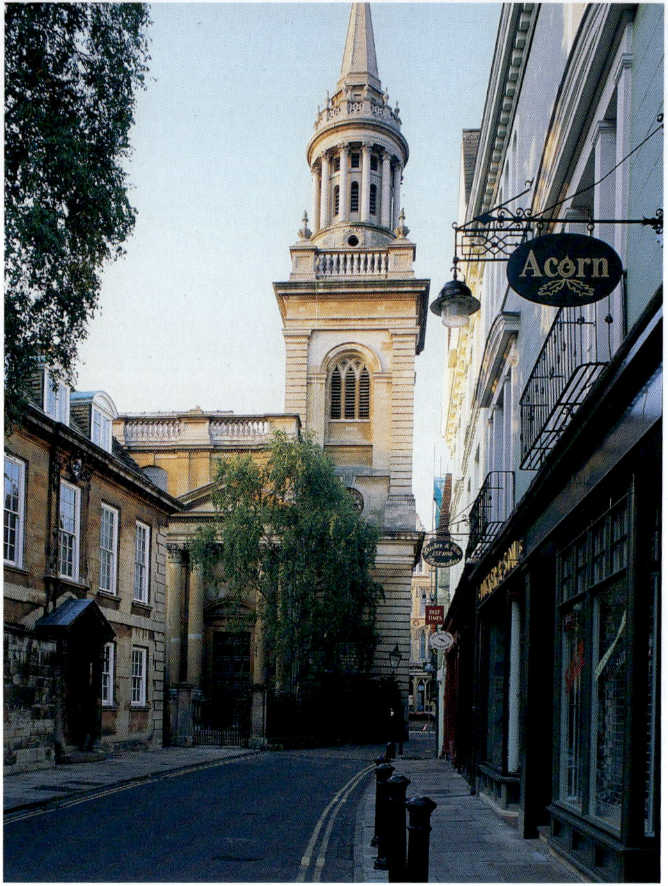

BLACKWELL'S BOOKSHOP
Broad Street

… Oxford is built upon books – books being read, books being written, books being published …

Jan Morris
Oxford
1965

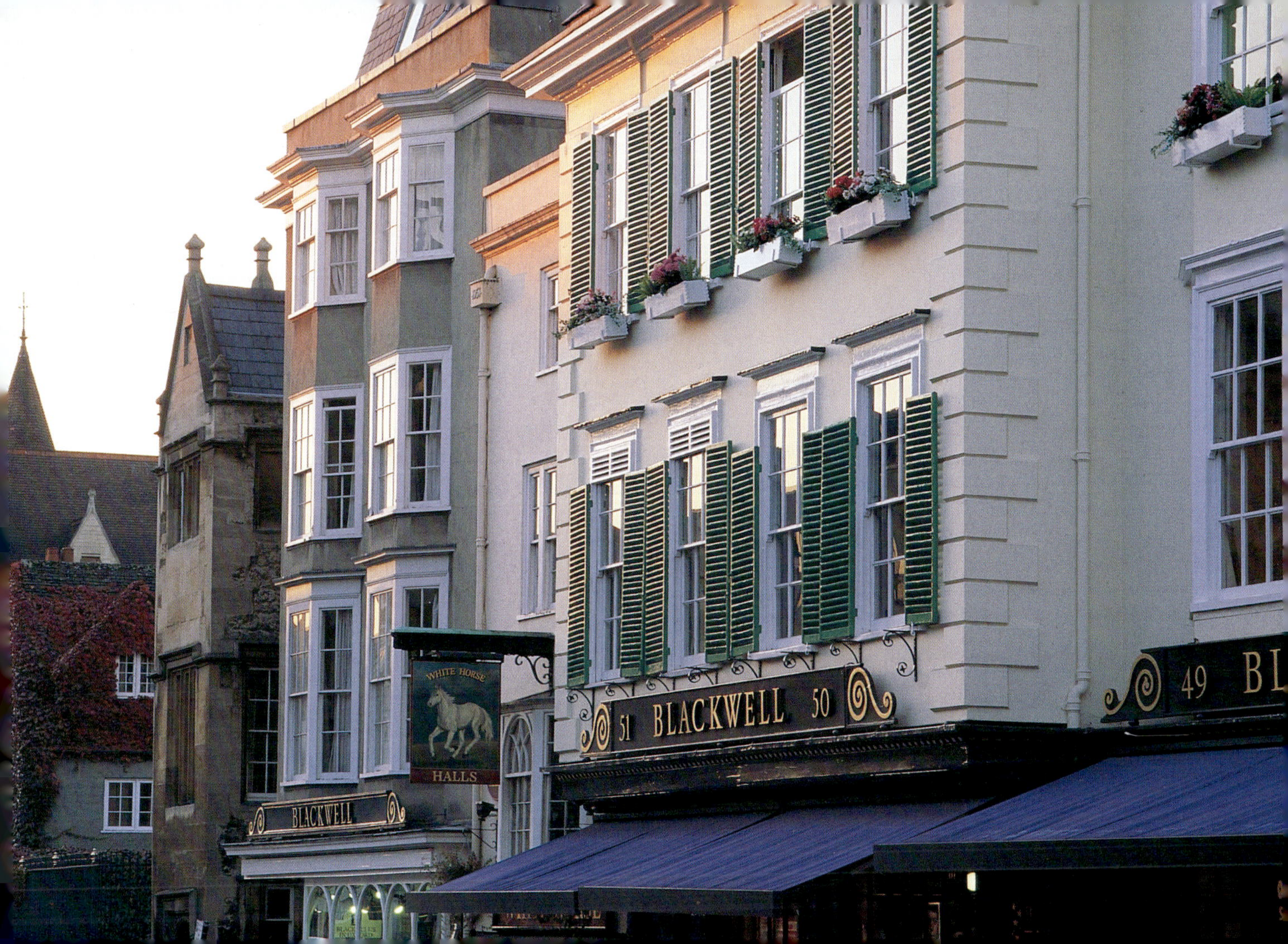

WHITE HORSE
HALLS
BLACKWELL
51 BLACKWELL 50
49 BL

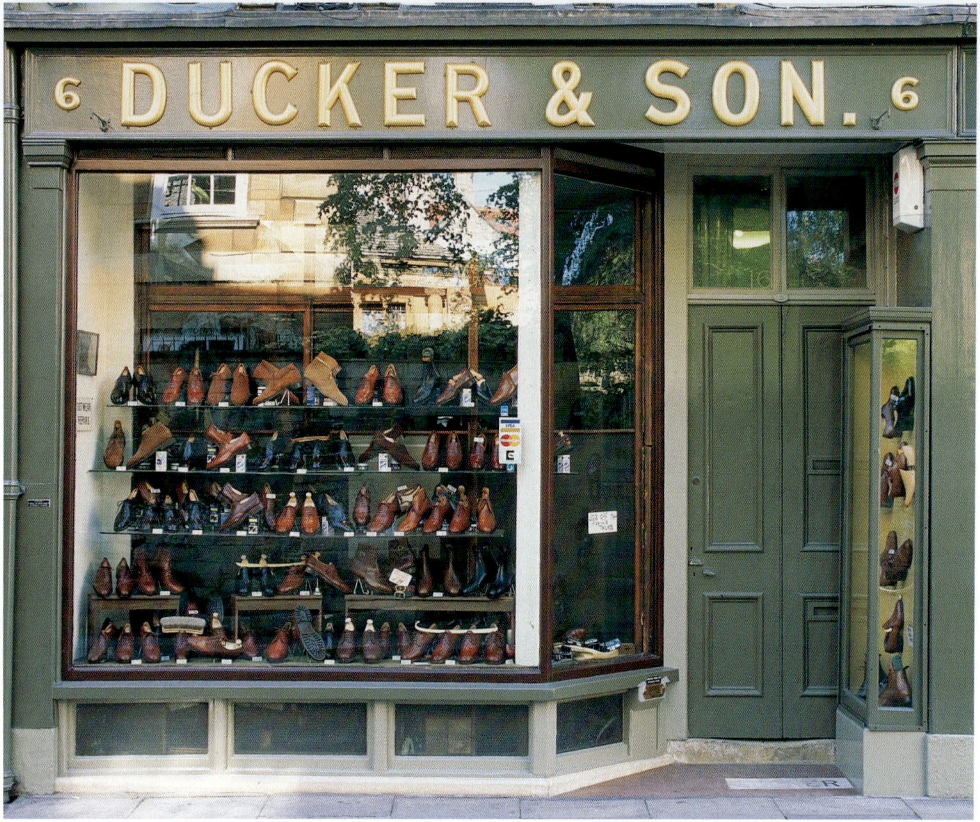

TURL STREET

Oxford … has bestowed its name on a strange assortment of objects, including Oxford sausages, Oxford marmalade, Oxford finger biscuits, Oxford ragweed, Oxford bags (trousers), Oxford shirting, Oxford grey … Oxford brogues, Oxford chairs … Oxford accent, Morris Oxford cars and other disparate subjects.

Christine G. Bloxham
Portrait of Oxfordshire
1982

Opened in 1898, Ducker & Son is the last survivor of Oxford's once numerous boot and shoe makers.

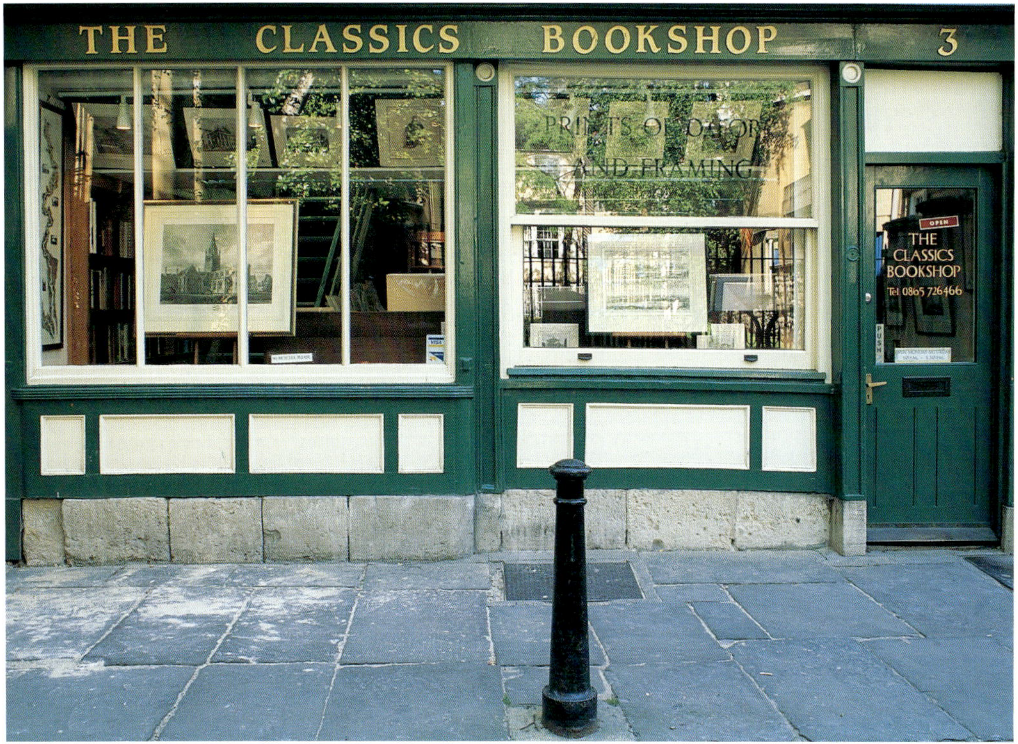

TURL STREET

… a bookshop, glowing like a jewel in the gloom of an ancient street lured him within. 'May I look round?' Michael asked. The bookseller nodded. 'Just come up?' he enquired.
'Today,' Michael confessed.
'And what sort of books are you interested in?'
'All books,' said Michael.

COMPTON MACKENZIE
Sinister Street
1913

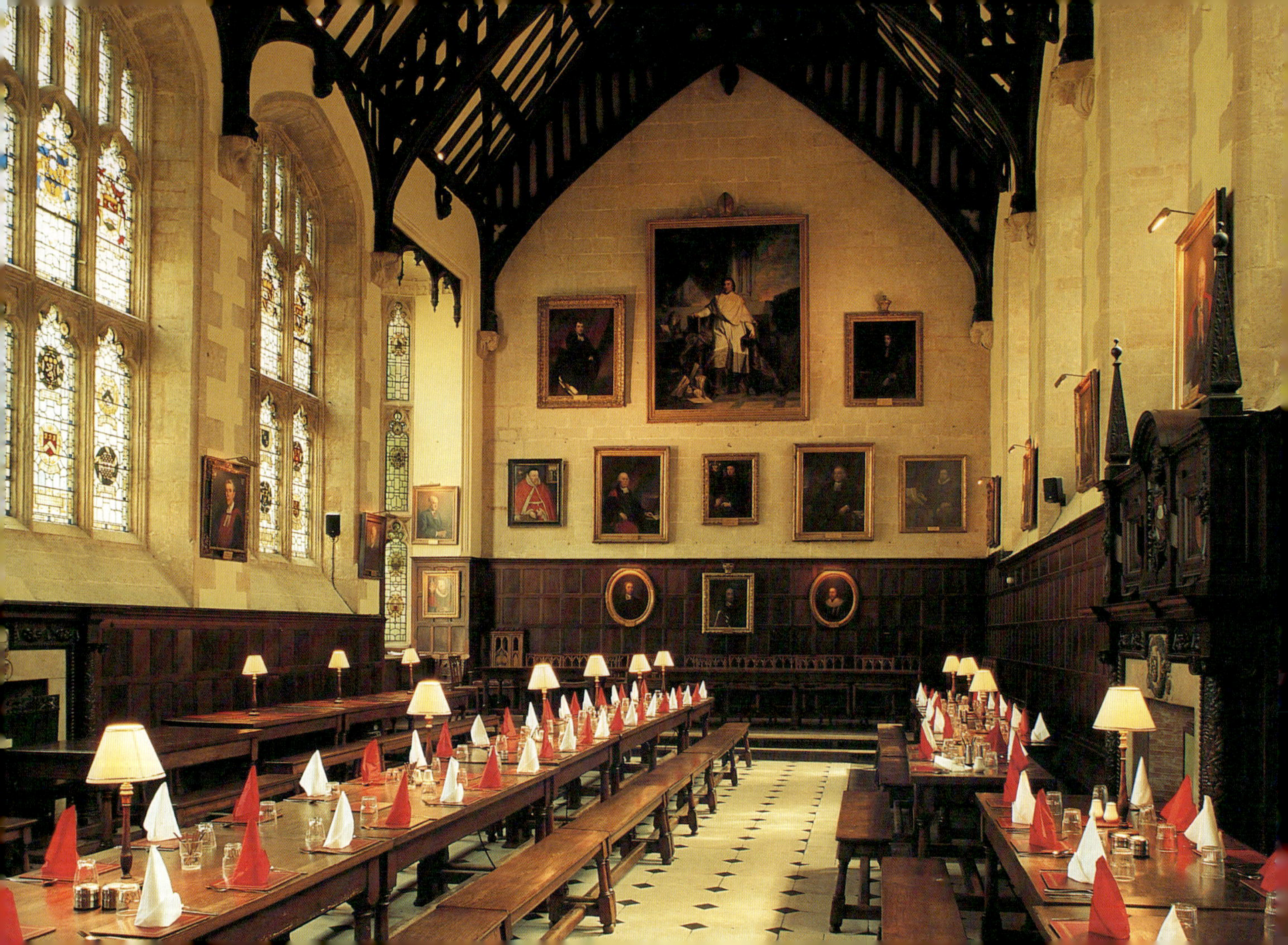

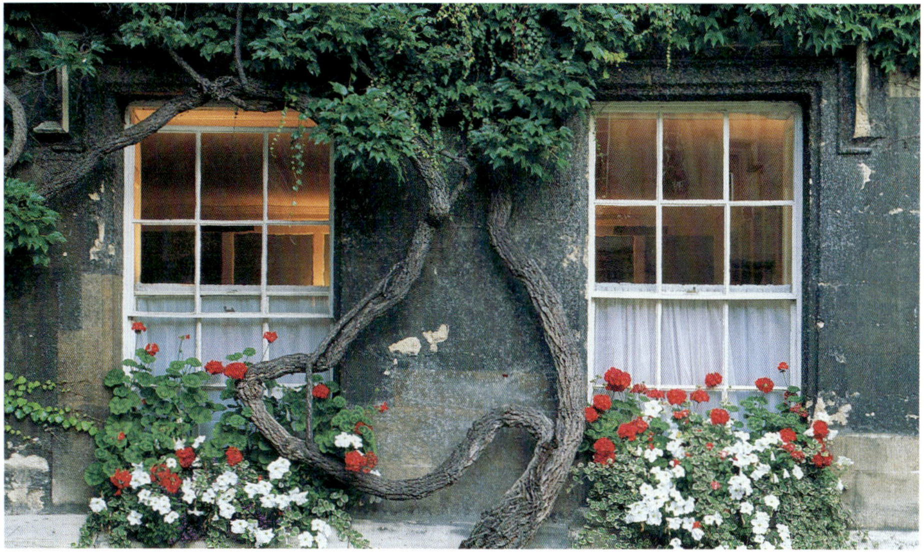

EXETER COLLEGE Hall

The hall of Exeter College is a fine example of the open timber-roofed buildings of the kind … It contains some remarkable portraits.

Ward Lock *Pictorial and Descriptive Guide to Oxford* 1894

LINCOLN COLLEGE Front Quad

Those old battlemented walls around the quadrangles; many gables; the windows with stone pavilions, so very antique, yet some of them adorned with fresh flowers in pots – a very sweet contrast; the ivy mantling the grey stone; and the infinite repose …

Nathaniel Hawthorne *English Notebooks* 1856

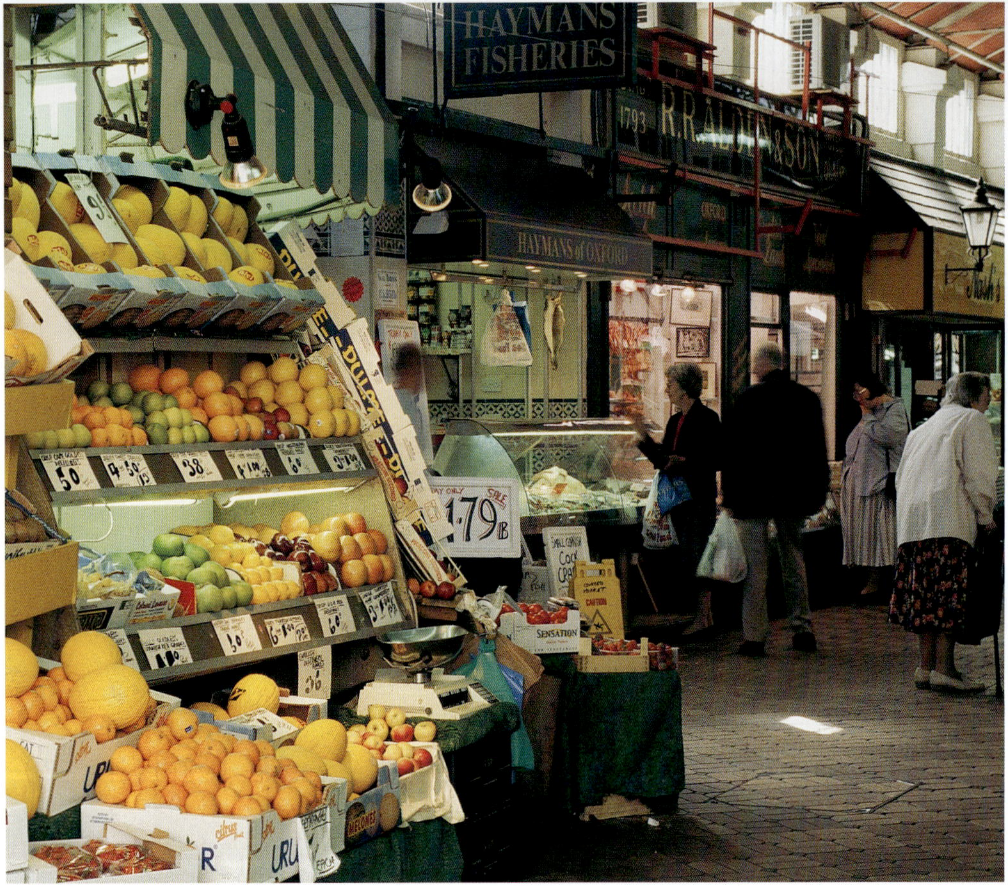

OXFORD COVERED MARKET
High Street

One of the last remnants of University control over the City now is the Assize of Butter, which allows the two University Clerks of the Market to pay a visit to the market, in company with an inspector of the police, and an assistant with scales and weights, and weigh any of the butter on sale; any under weight being at once confiscated. This is actually done once or twice every term …

Henry W. Taunt
Oxford: Illustrated by Camera and Pen
1911

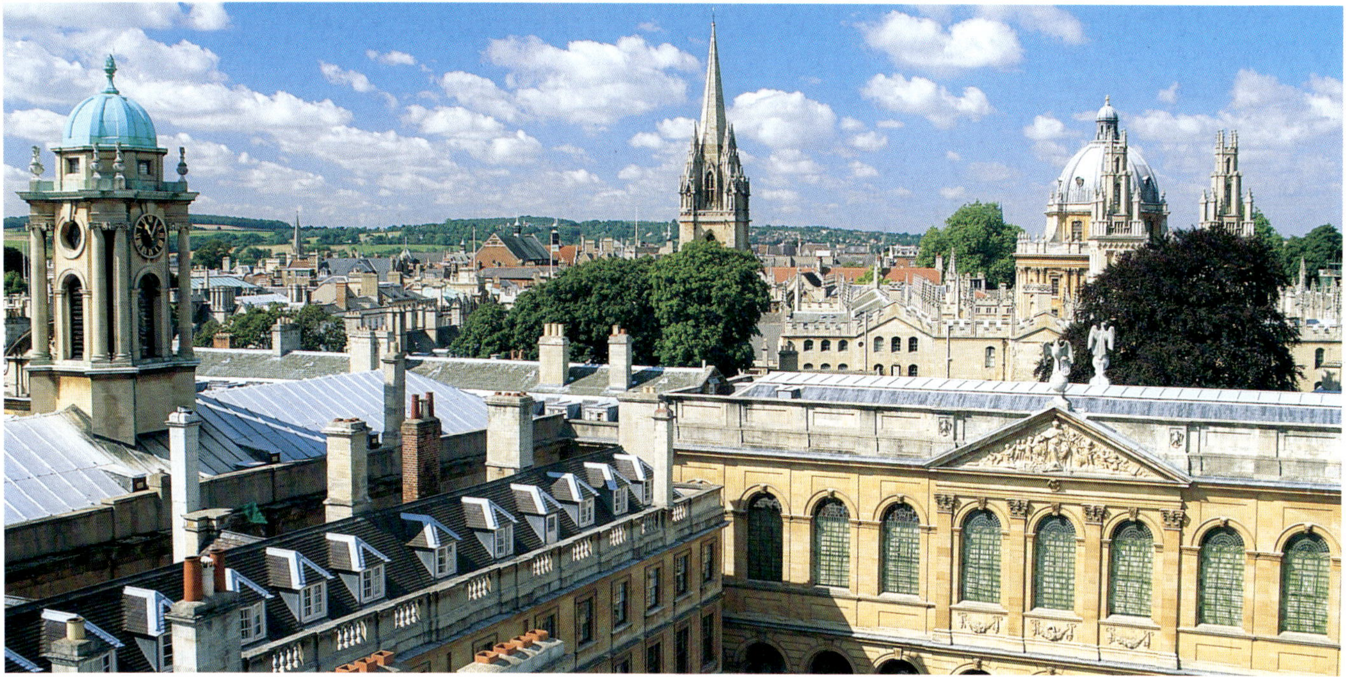

OXFORD FROM THE LIBRARY TOWER OF ST EDMUND HALL

Oxford, my passion … the whole air of the town charms me.

HORACE WALPOLE *Letter to Richard Bentley, September 1753*

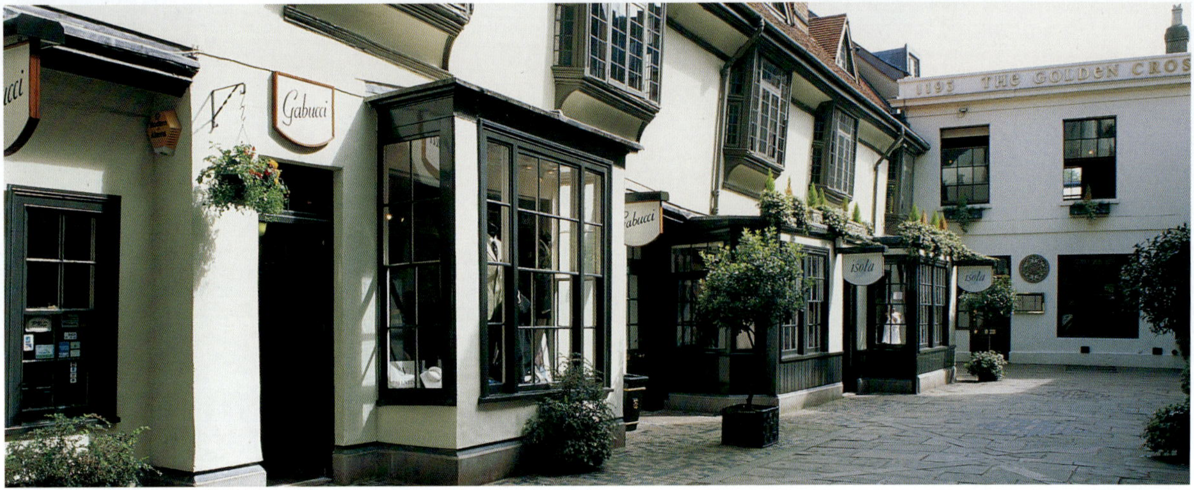

GOLDEN CROSS Cornmarket Street

There are now not many spots in England, apart from landscape viewpoints, where a man may say with reasonable conviction: 'Shakespeare stood here and saw this.' Most of them are in Oxford. One is the Painted Room at No. 3 Cornmarket; another is the timbered archway of the Golden Cross with the courtyard on which it opened.

E. A. Greening Lambourn *The Golden Cross: Seven Centuries of an Oxford Inn* 1948

THE MITRE High Street

You will hear more good things on the outside of a stagecoach from London to Oxford than if you were to pass a twelvemonth with the Undergraduates, or Heads of College, of that famous university.

William Hazlitt *On the Ignorance of the Learned* 1821

The Mitre was once a coaching inn.

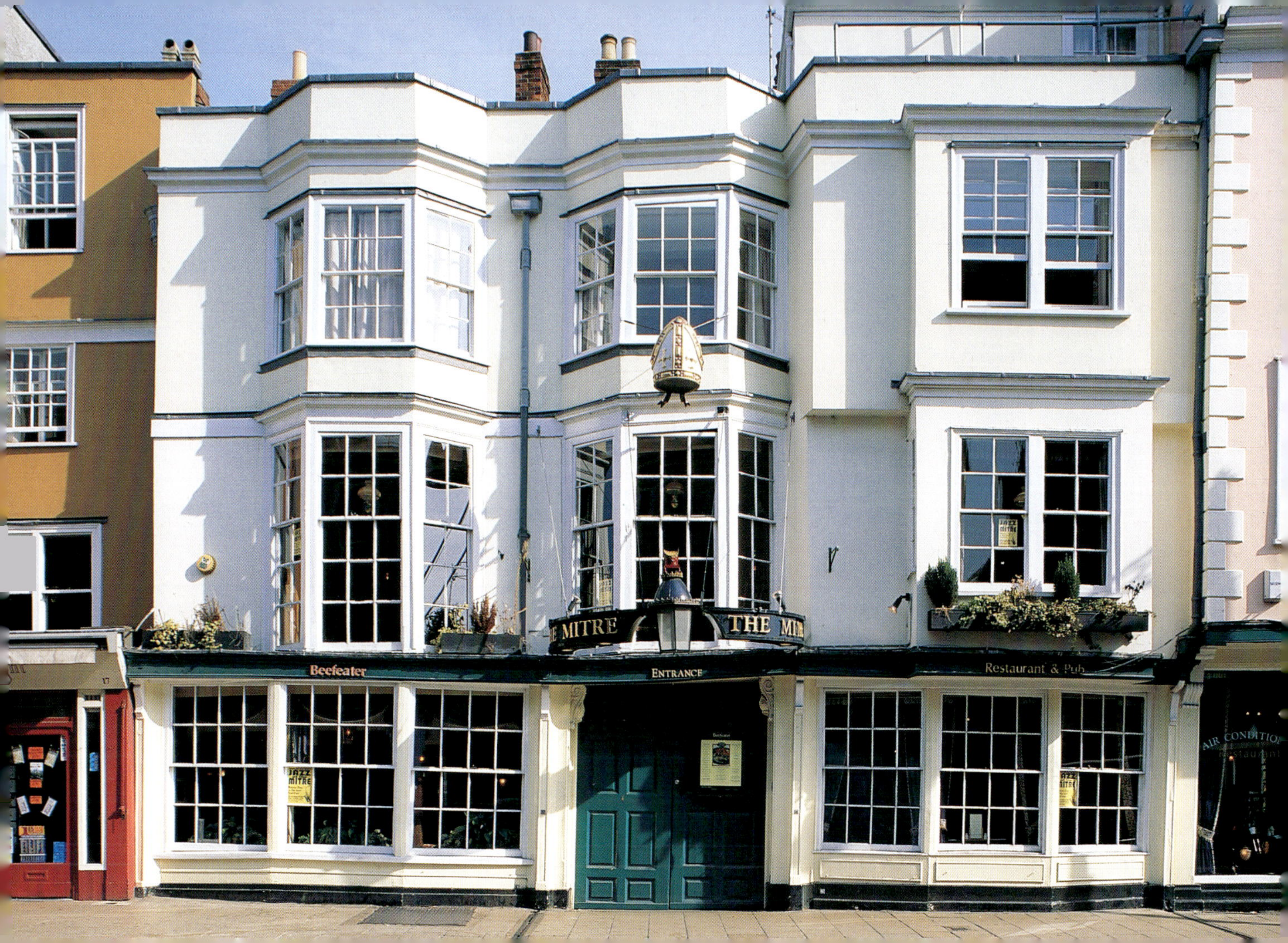

THE MITRE
Beefeater
ENTRANCE
Restaurant & Pub
JAZZ MITRE

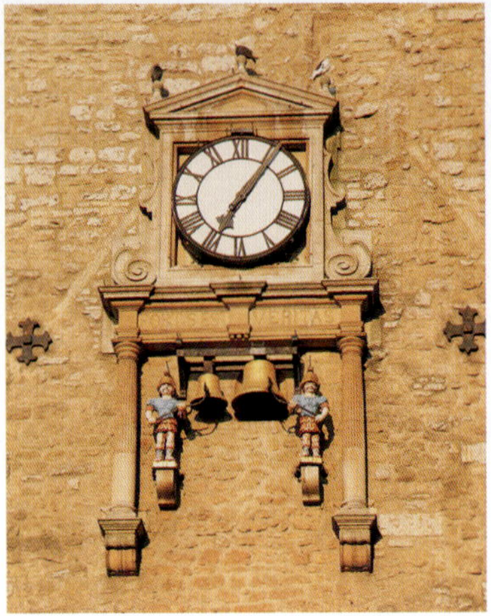

CARFAX

At Fourways [Carfax] men had stood and talked of Napoleon, the loss of America, the execution of King Charles, the burning of the Martyrs, the Crusades, the Norman Conquest, possibly of the arrival of Caesar.

THOMAS HARDY
Jude the Obscure
1896

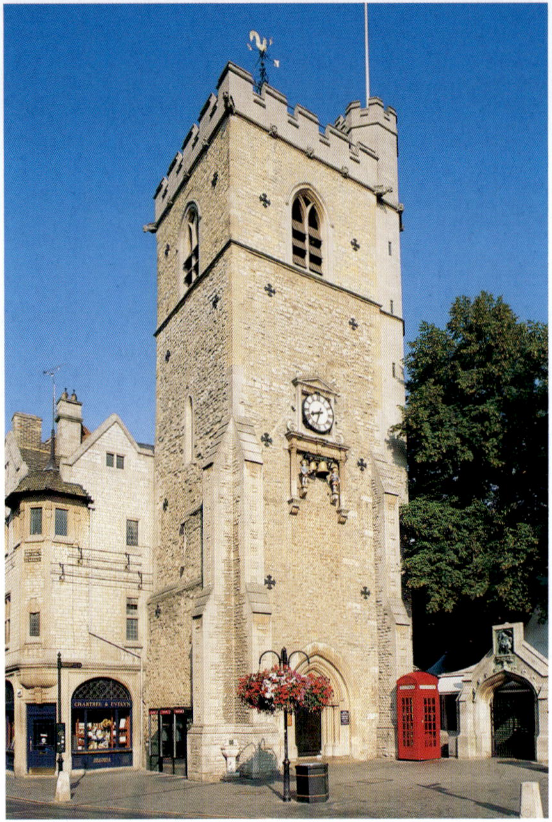

RANDOLPH HOTEL
BEAUMONT STREET

... the 'Randolph' always claimed to be smarter and more superior than its rivals, advertising itself at the turn of the century as 'The only *modern-built* hotel in Oxford, with Ladies' Coffee Room, Night Porter and *American Elevator*'.

HAL CHEETHAM
Portrait of Oxford
1971

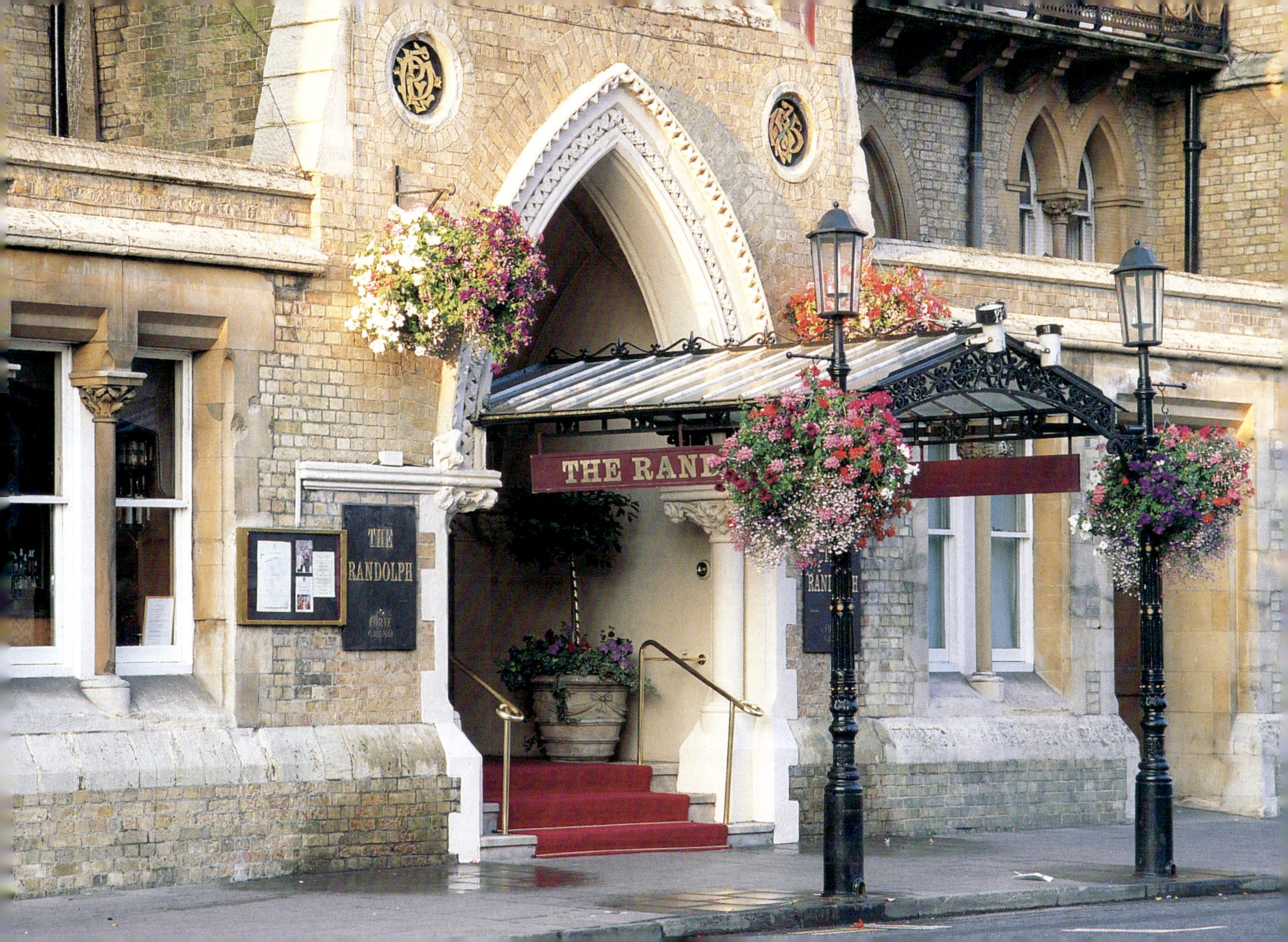
THE RAND
THE
RANDOLPH

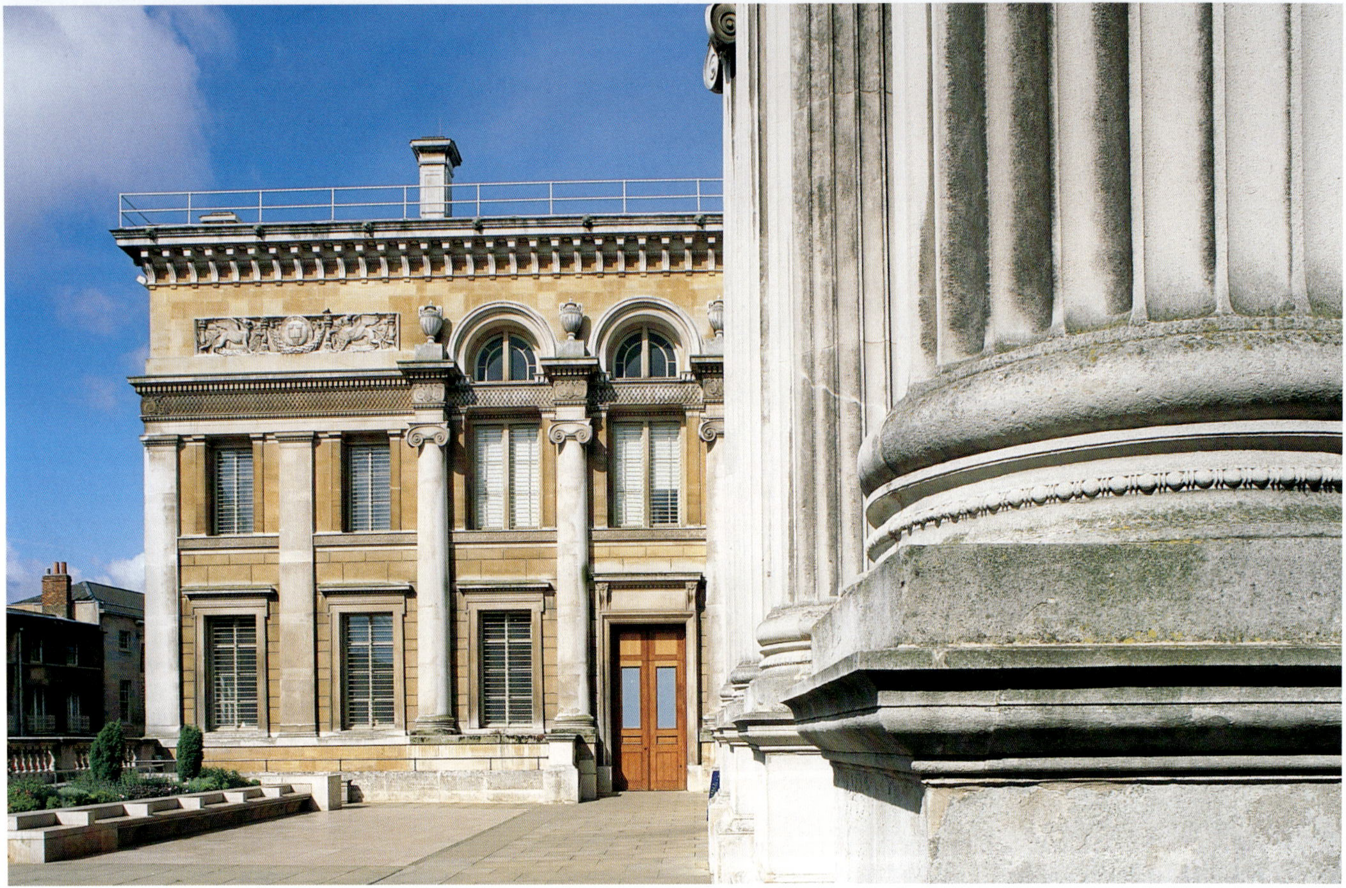

ASHMOLEAN MUSEUM
Beaumont Street

… I started my second year by joining the Ruskin School of Art; two or three mornings a week we met, about a dozen of us – half, at least, the daughters of North Oxford – among the casts from the antique at the Ashmolean Museum …

Evelyn Waugh
Brideshead Revisited
1945

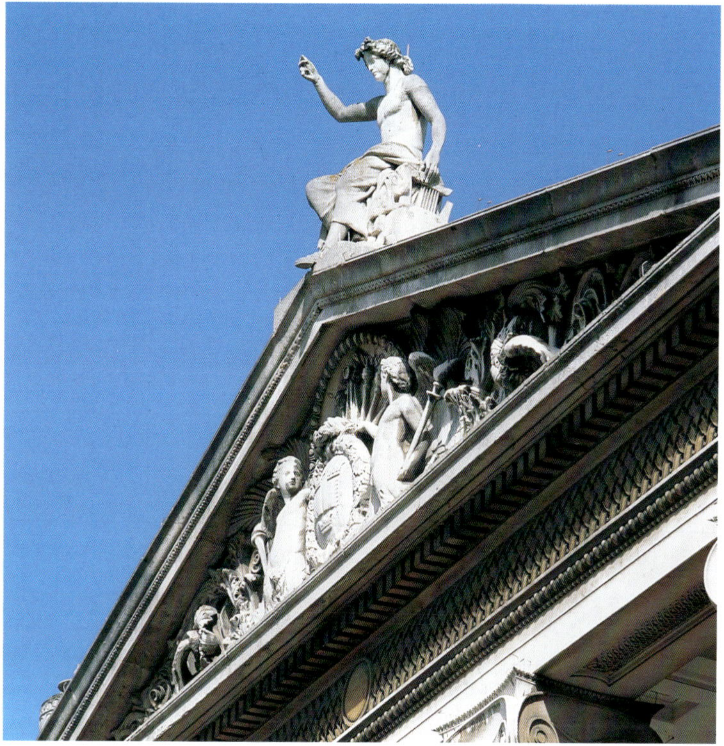

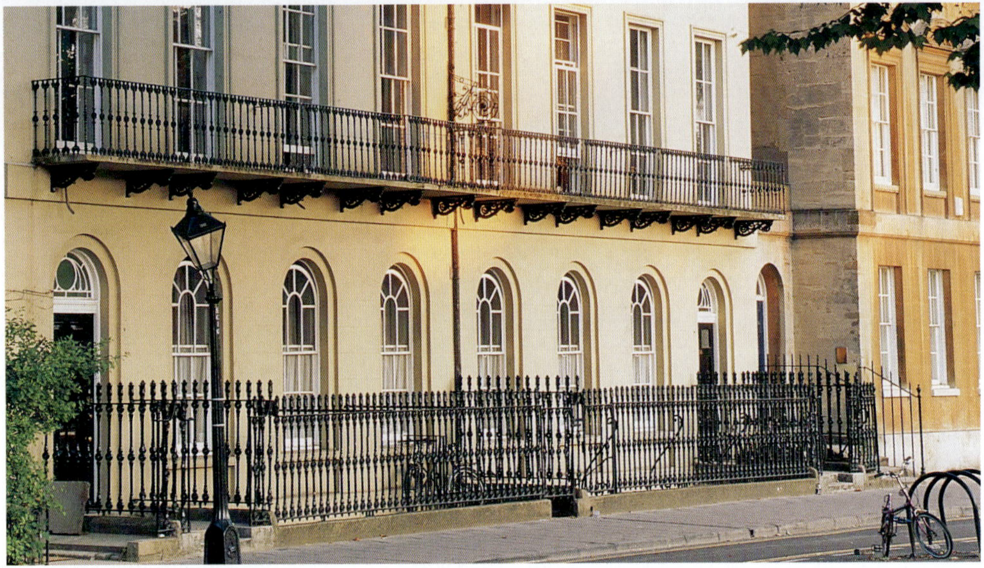

ST GILES

St Giles … can claim something of nobility. It is also the nearest thing that Oxford has to a monumental Renaissance vista-street. It is almost straight: it is wide: it has an avenue of trees … St Giles shows us, as High Street does, that nobility need not be pompous, and that, in an architectural sense, a pub may be a very suitable neighbour to a (collegiate) palace.

THOMAS SHARP *Oxford Observed* 1952

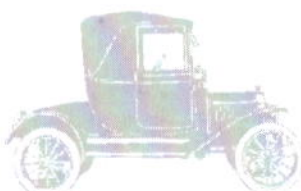

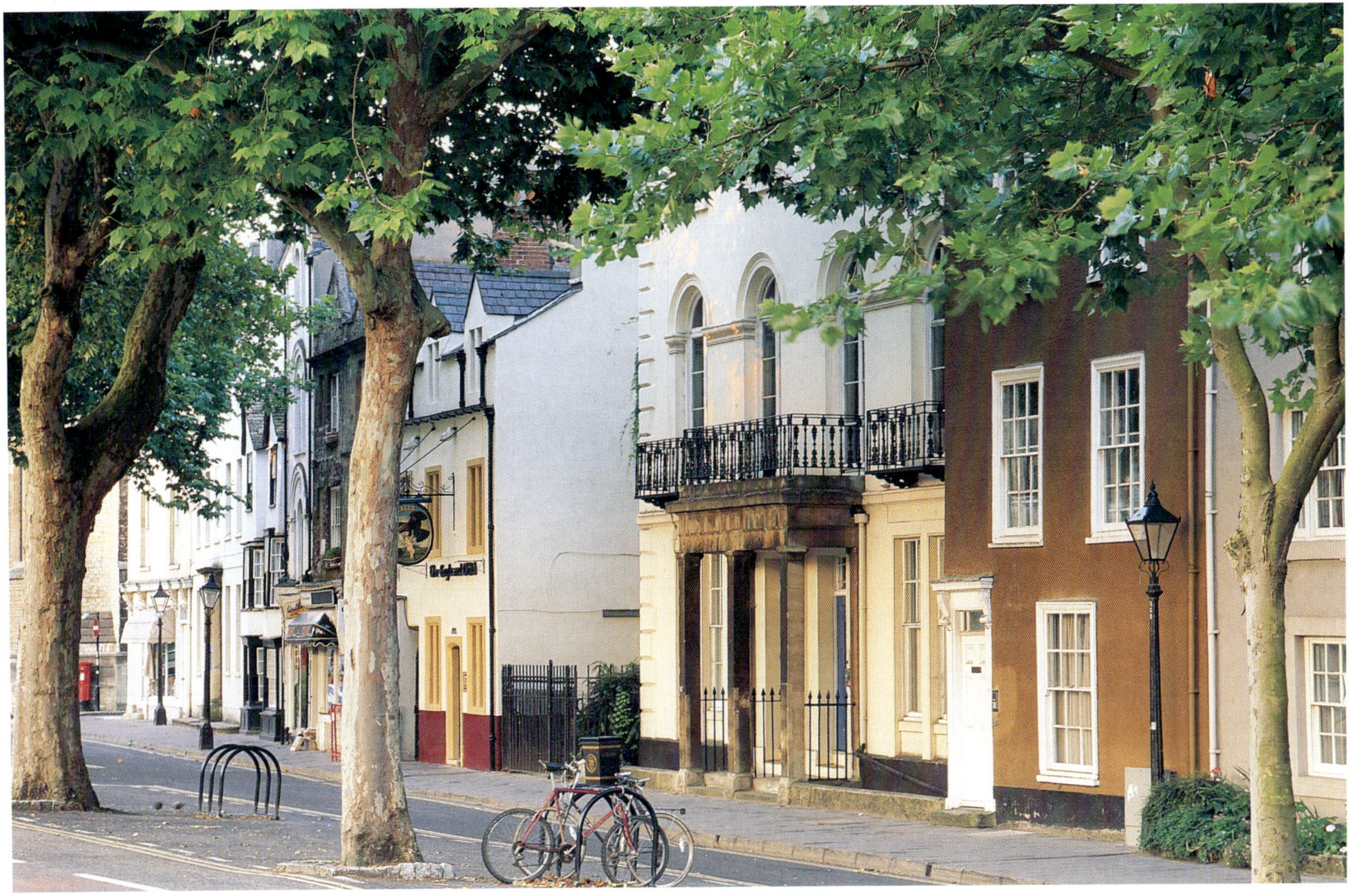

EAGLE AND CHILD
ST GILES

This curiously named inn dates from about 1650, the sign being derived from the arms of the Earl of Derby. Colloquially known as the 'Bird and Baby', it was used as the meeting place by 'The Inklings', a group of writers which included C. S. Lewis and J. R. R. Tolkien, and is much frequented by fans of *The Hobbit*. A landlady once kept rabbits in the third bar, which is still referred to as 'The Rabbit Room.'

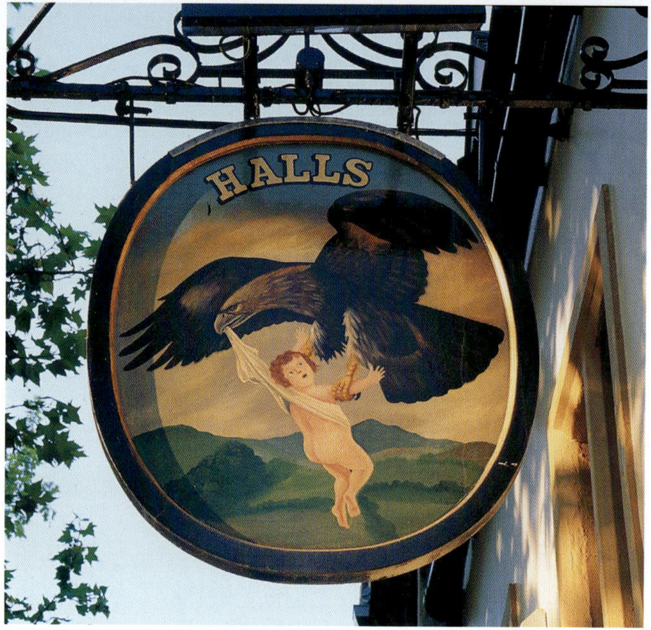

ST CROSS COLLEGE

The buildings, the work of Mr Temple Moore, are perhaps the best constructed in Oxford in modern times, and it is very notable and refreshing that in a place where there is so much drab imitation of Gothic, there is at last erected in that style something original and inspired.

L. RICE-OXLEY
Oxford Renowned
1925

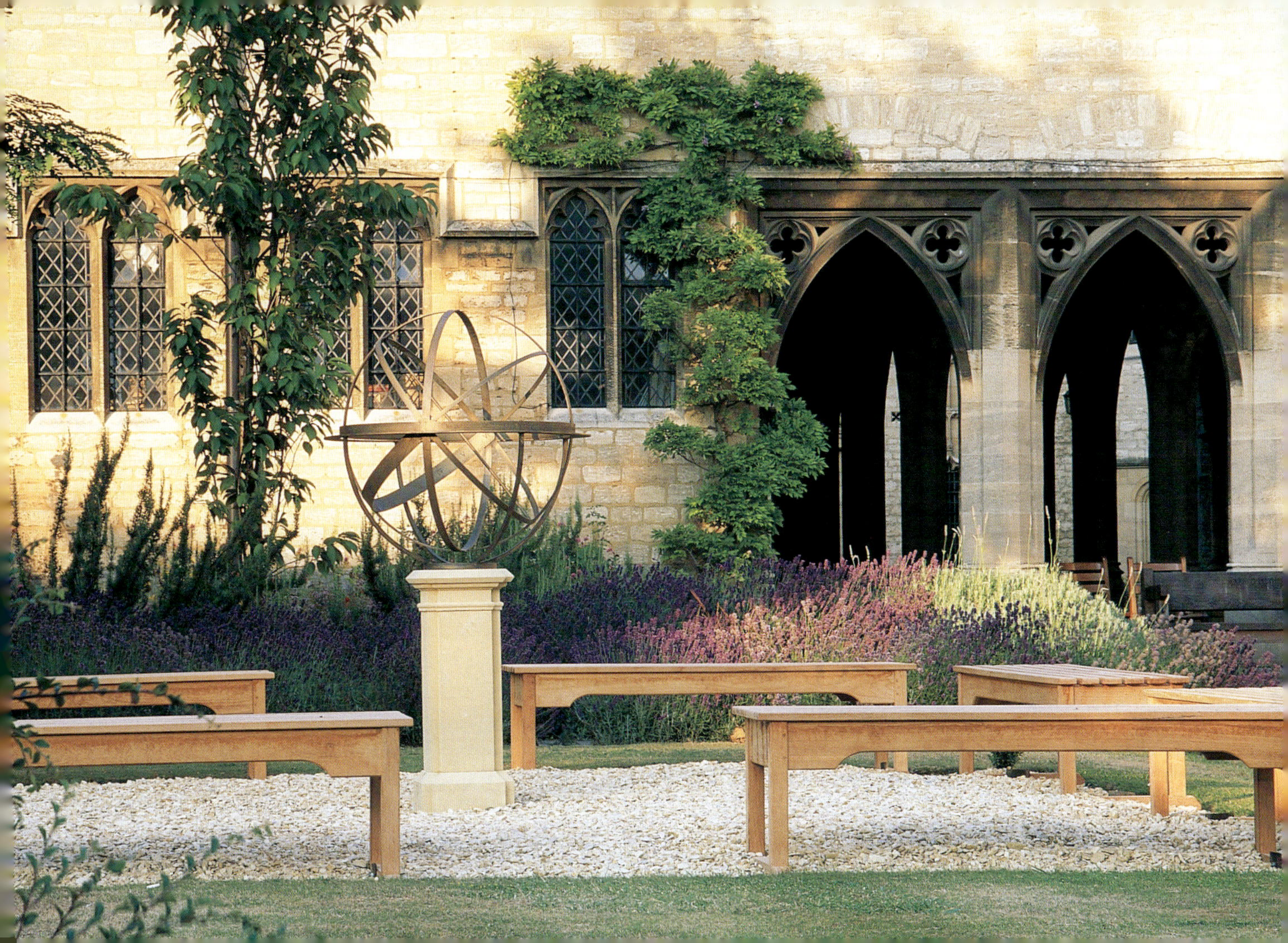

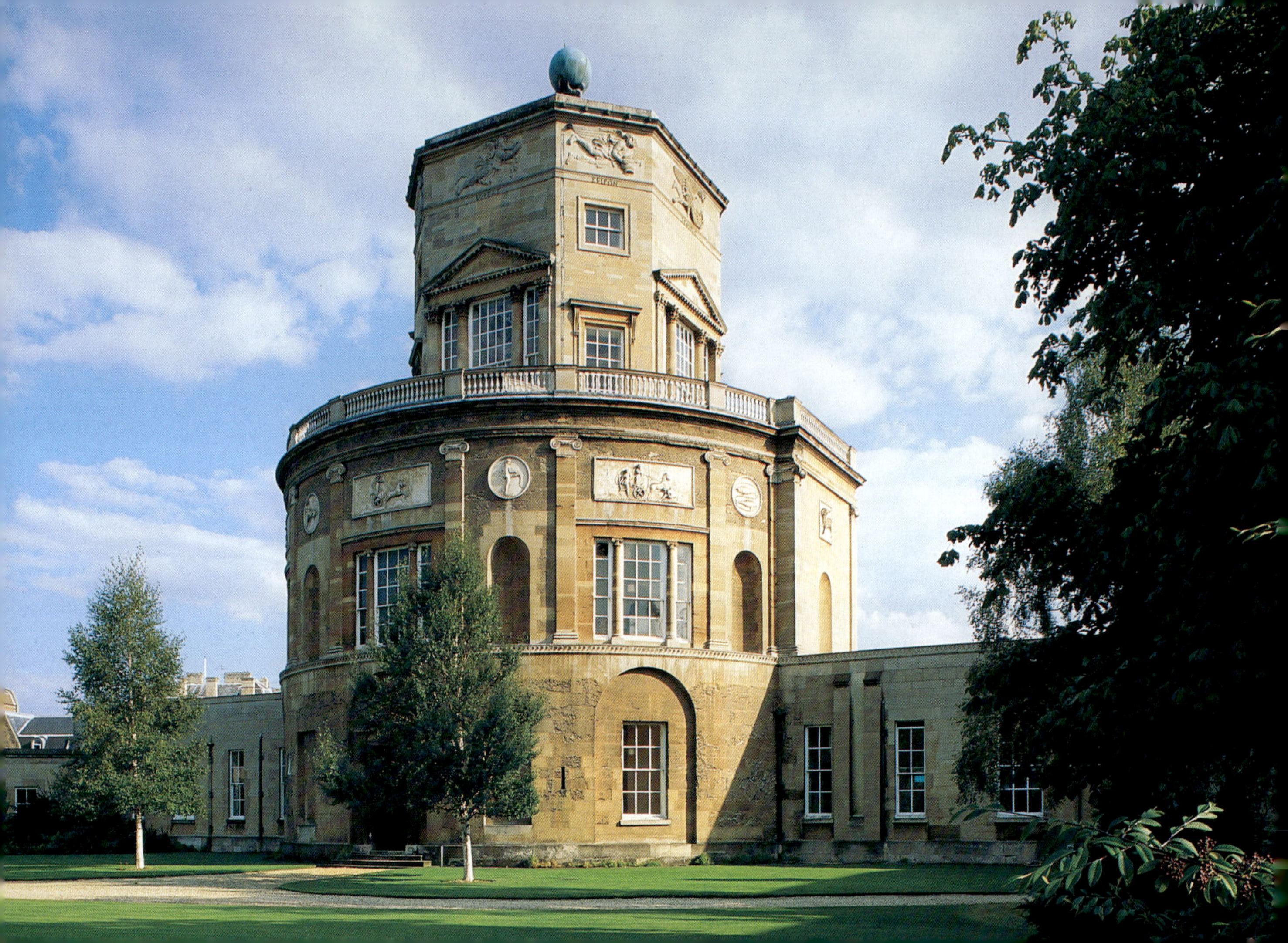

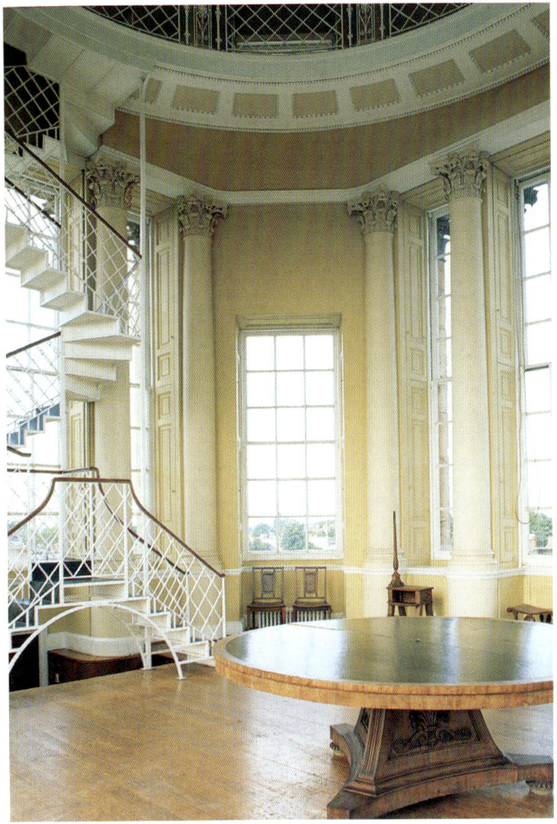

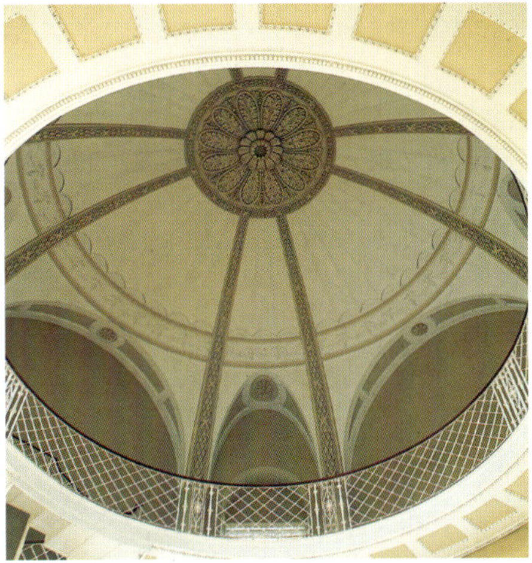

GREEN TEMPLETON COLLEGE
Radcliffe Observatory

Until its change of use, at the start of each Michaelmas term the *University Gazette* carried this notice: 'The Director of the University Observatory gives notice that on fine and clear Thursday evenings in the Michaelmas and Hilary terms between 8 and 10 p.m. celestial objects will be shown through the telescope to members of the University and friends accompanying them.'

Alec Clifton-Taylor *Buildings of Delight* 1986

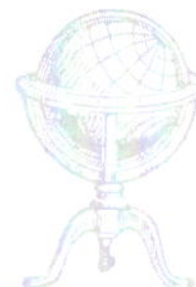

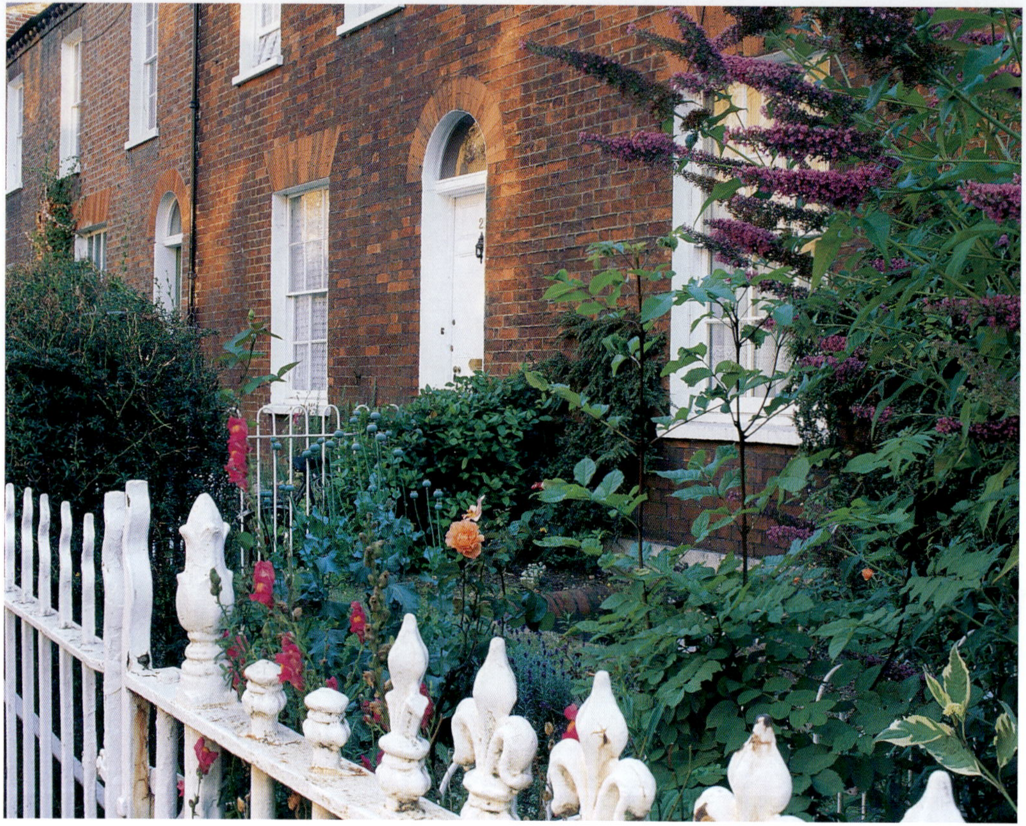

JERICHO
Walton Street

The origin of the curious name of this area, lying between St Giles and the canal, is obscure. Some have suggested that the whistling of engines on the nearby railway would bring down the walls of the humble dwellings; others that it was Oxford's Jewish quarter. The terraced houses, once occupied by Victorian artisans, have been progressively improved making this a desirable area of the city.

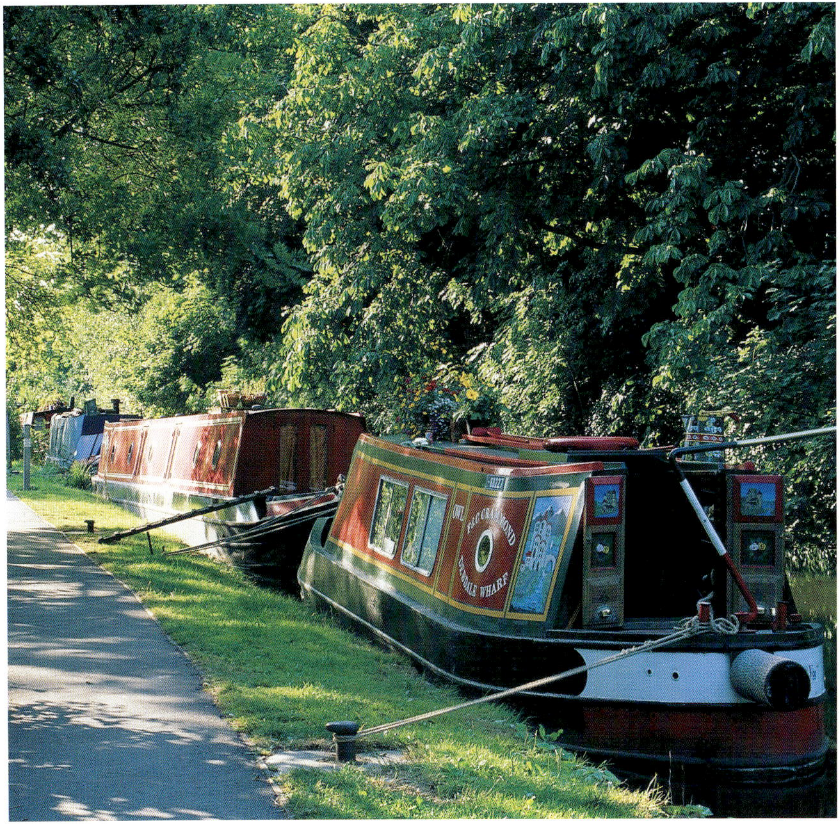

OXFORD CANAL
NEAR HYTHE BRIDGE STREET

When you have wearied of the valiant spires
  of this County Town,
Of its wide white streets and glistening
  museums, and black monastic walls,
Of its red motors and lumbering trams,
  and self sufficient people,
I will take you walking with me to a place
  you have not seen –
Half town and half country – the land of
  the Canal.
Straightest, sublimest of rivers is the
  long Canal.
I have observed great storms and trembled:
  I have wept for fear of the dark.
But nothing makes me so afraid as the clear
  water of this idle canal on a summer's noon.

JAMES ELROY FLECKER
From 'Oxford Canal'

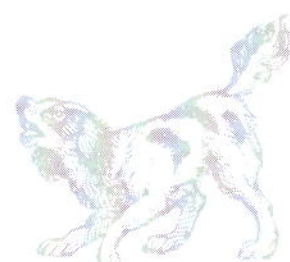

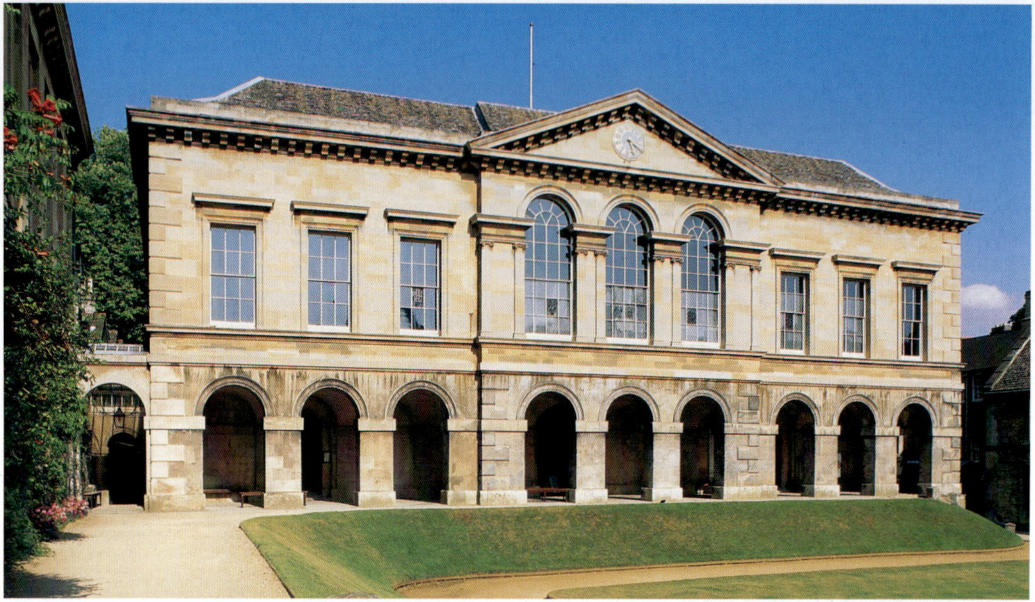

WORCESTER COLLEGE Main Quad

Worcester College was founded in 1714 and incorporates buildings of the medieval Gloucester College. Because of its distance from the city centre at that time it was known as 'Botany Bay'.

WORCESTER COLLEGE Cloister

Life at Oxford is the very curious mixture of a cloistered but extremely pleasant microcosm and sudden glimpses of a bigger world outside.

Theodore Andrea Cook *The Sunlit Hours: a Record of Sport and Life* 1925

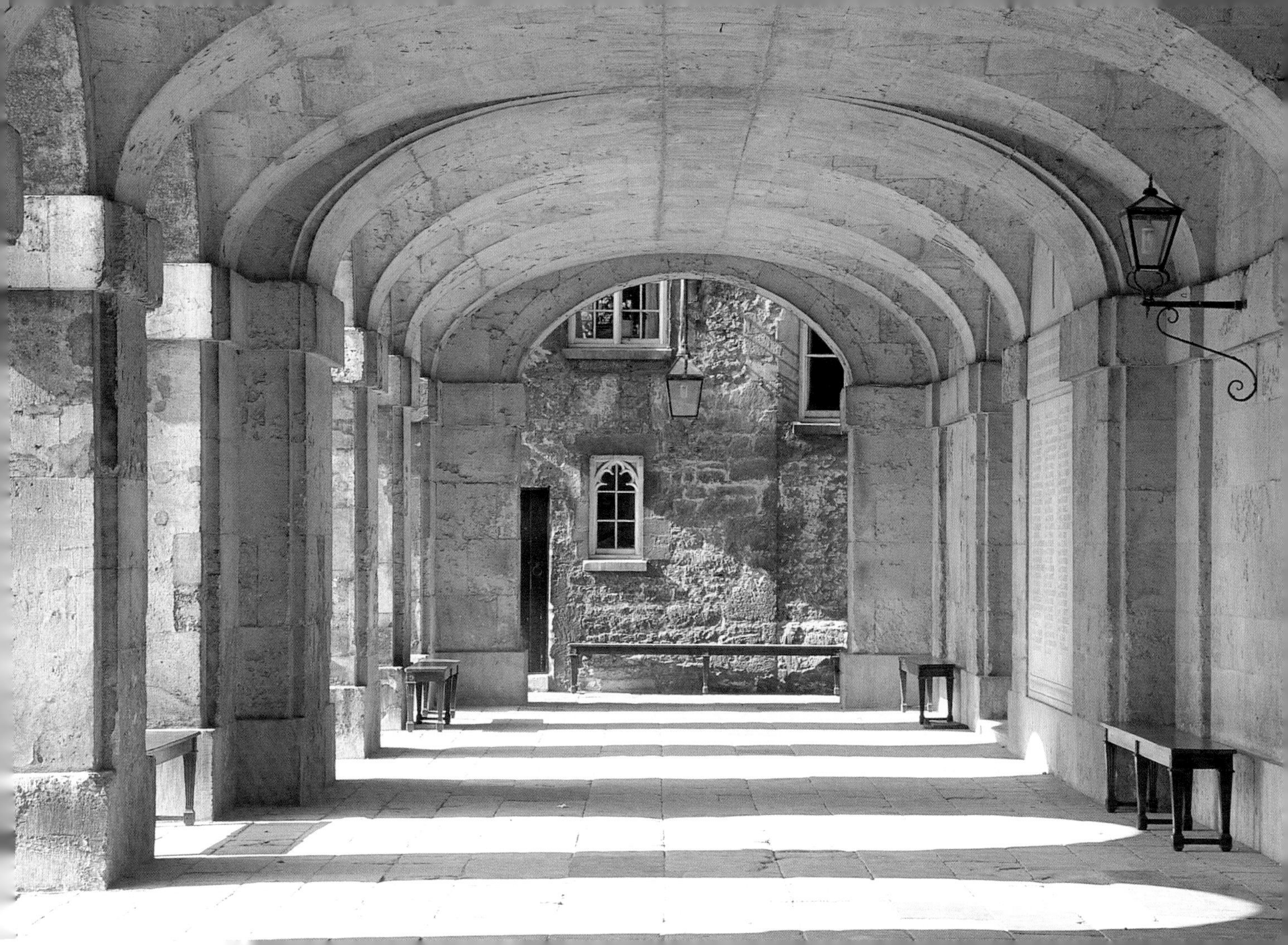

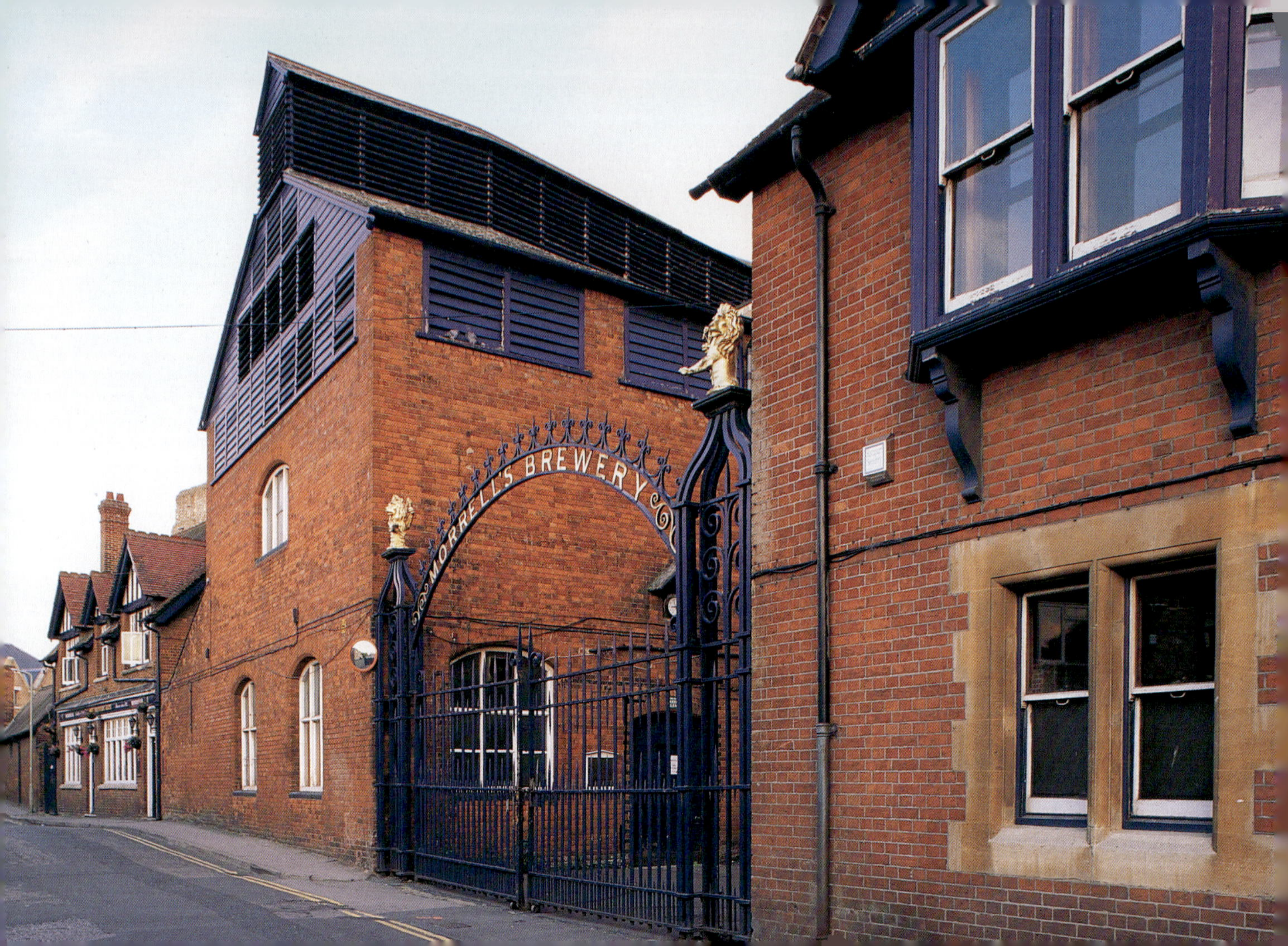
MORRELL'S BREWERY

MORRELL'S BREWERY
St Thomas' Street

In Oxford the brewing of beer has a long history. Many of the colleges had their own breweries and the monks of Osney brewed beer commercially at least as early as the 15th century. It is said that the rivalry between 'town and gown' originated with student anger at the prices charged by the town's alehouses. Brewing was carried out on this site since at least 1563 and was in the hands of the Morrell family from the beginning of the 19th century until 1998 when the brewery closed. The brewery buildings have been converted into offices and apartments.

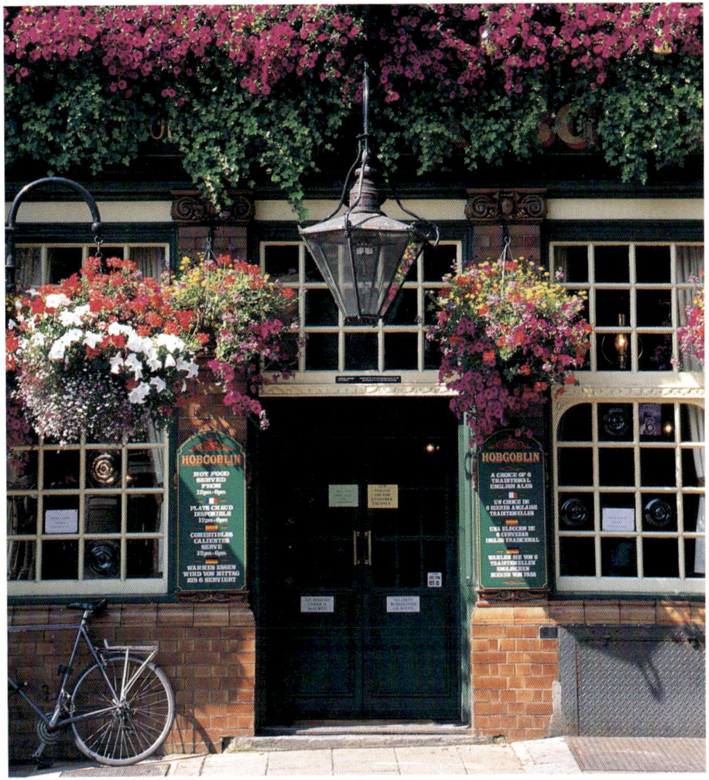

HOBGOBLIN
St Aldates

Oxford had at least taught me to drink pint by pint with any man.

Graham Greene
A Sort of Life
1971

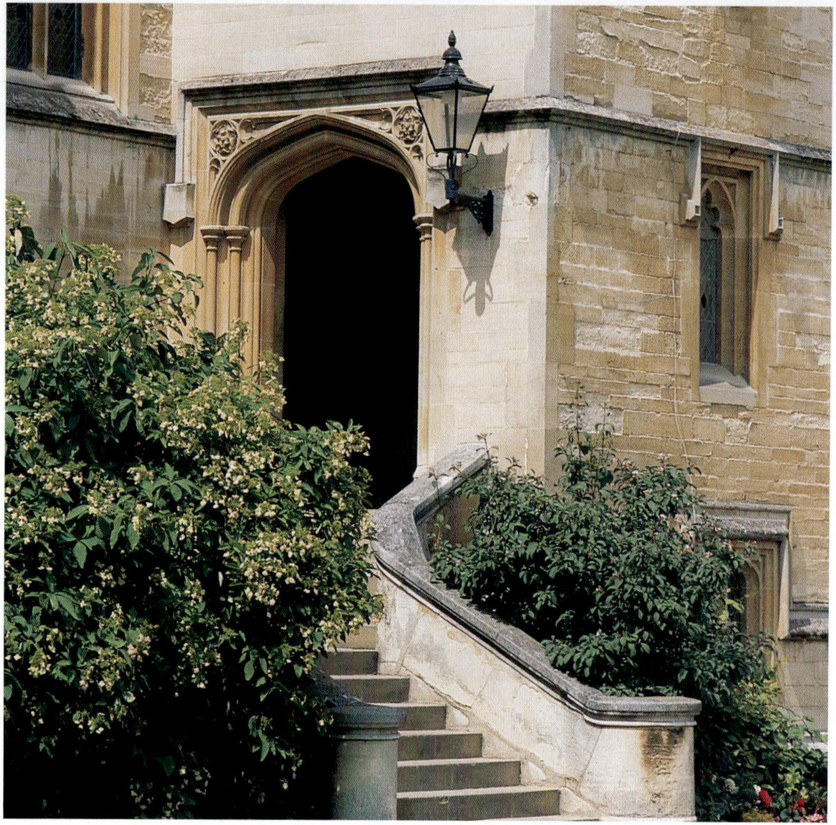

PEMBROKE COLLEGE

[Dr Johnson] took pleasure in boasting of the many eminent men who had been educated at Pembroke ... Being himself a poet, Johnson was peculiarly happy in mentioning how many of the sons of Pembroke were poets; adding, with a smile of sportive triumph, 'Sir, we are a nest of singing birds.'

JAMES BOSWELL
The Life of Samuel Johnson
1791

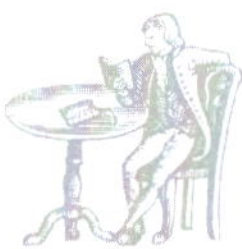

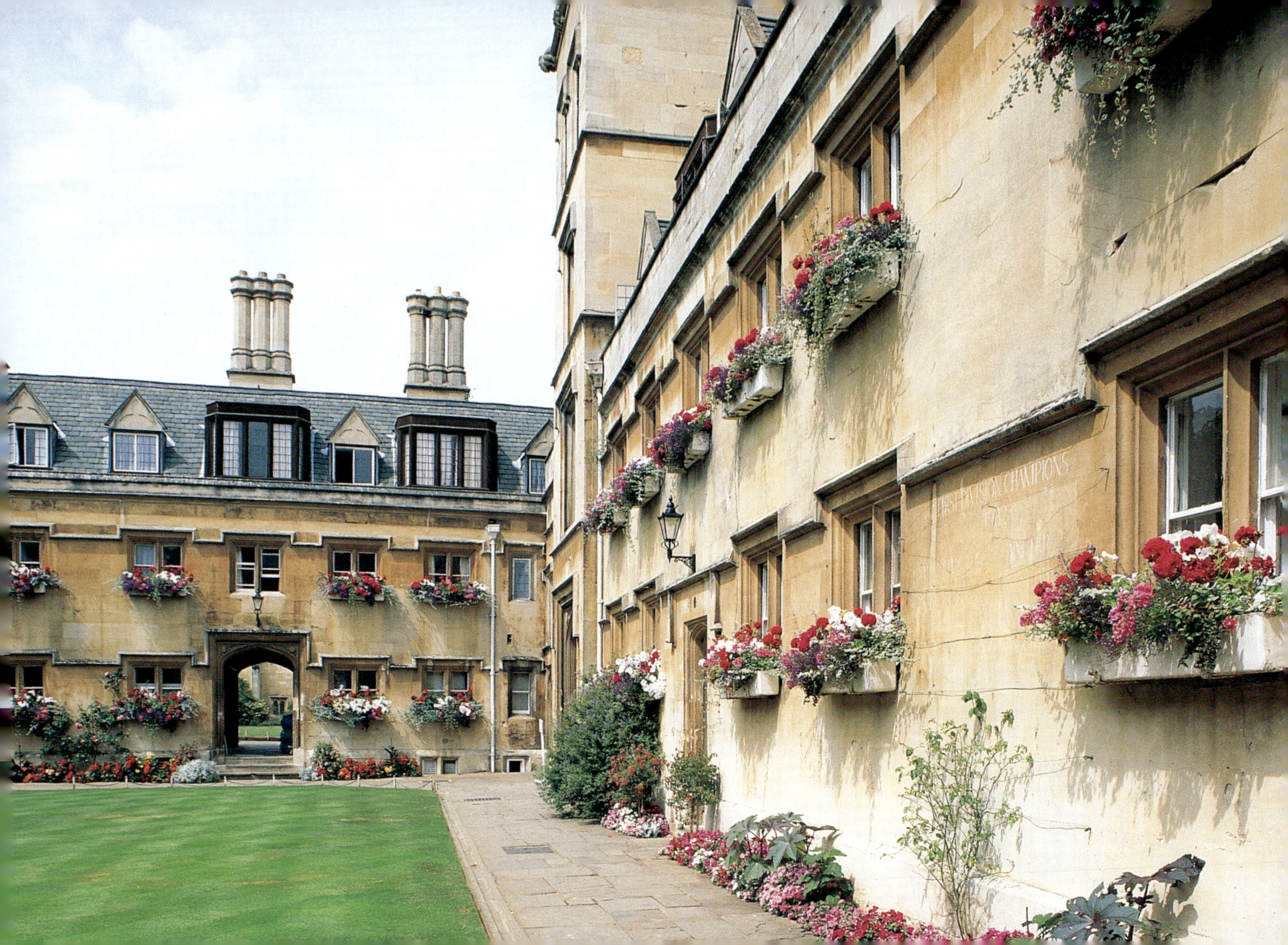
FIRST DIVISION CHAMPIONS

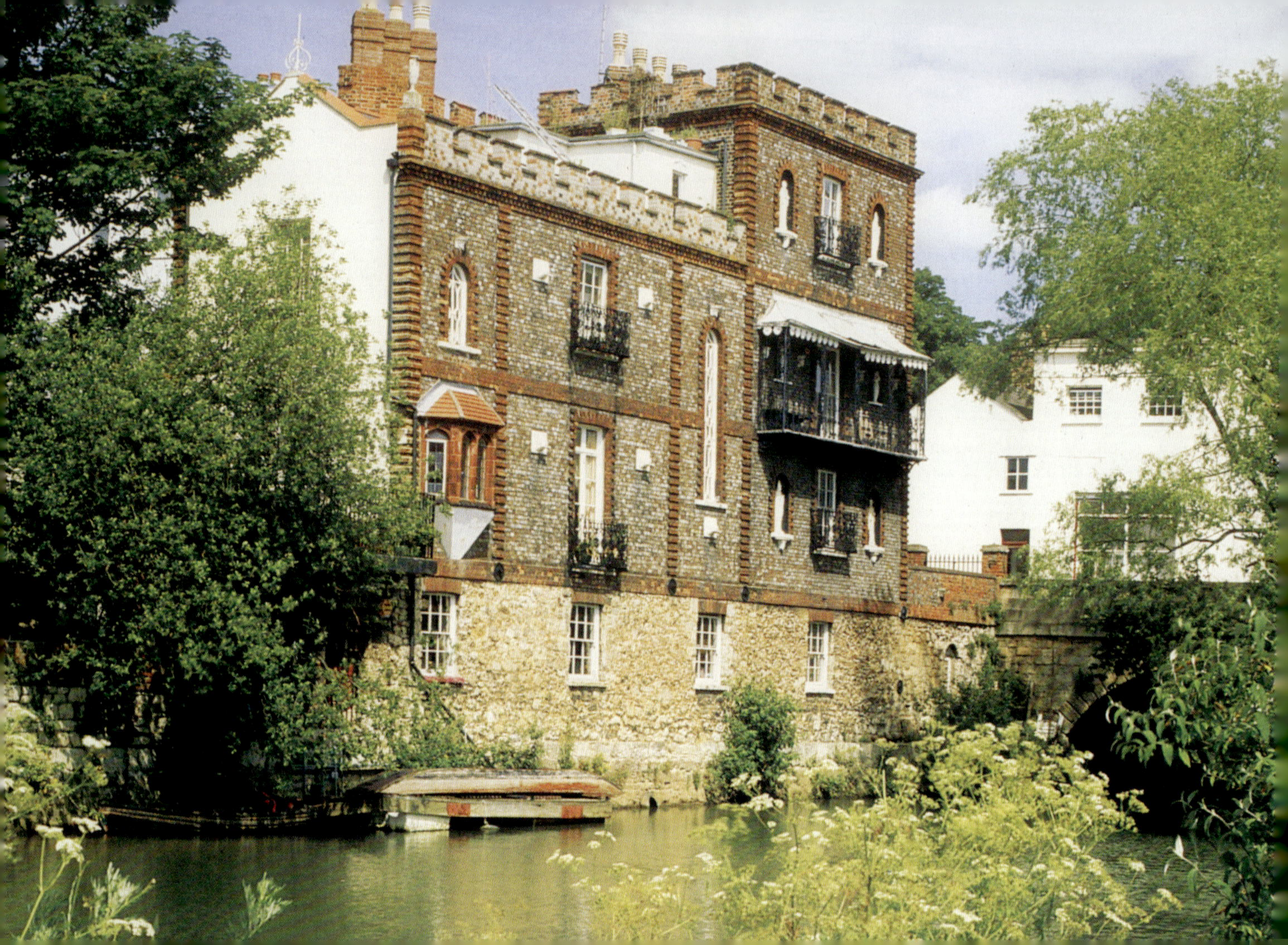

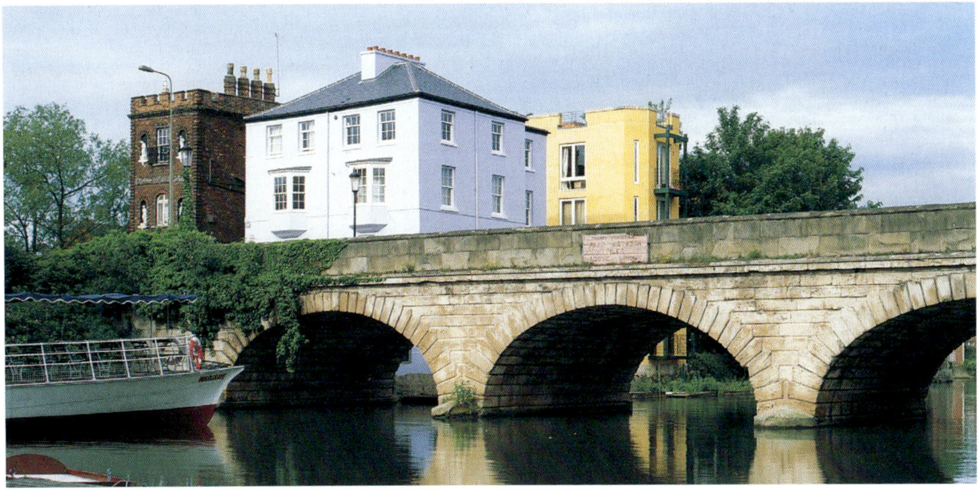

ISIS HOUSE *left,* AND FOLLY BRIDGE *above*

… built in 1849 by Joseph Cauldwell, an eccentric accountant, who wanted the house built as a castle to withstand attacks made by rioting undergraduates, a perpetual fear of his. As is so often the case, it was Cauldwell who proved to be the aggressor, shooting and severely wounding a student who had tried to make off with one of his brass cannons.

Gwyn Headley and Wim Meulenkamp *Follies, Grottoes and Garden Buildings* 1999

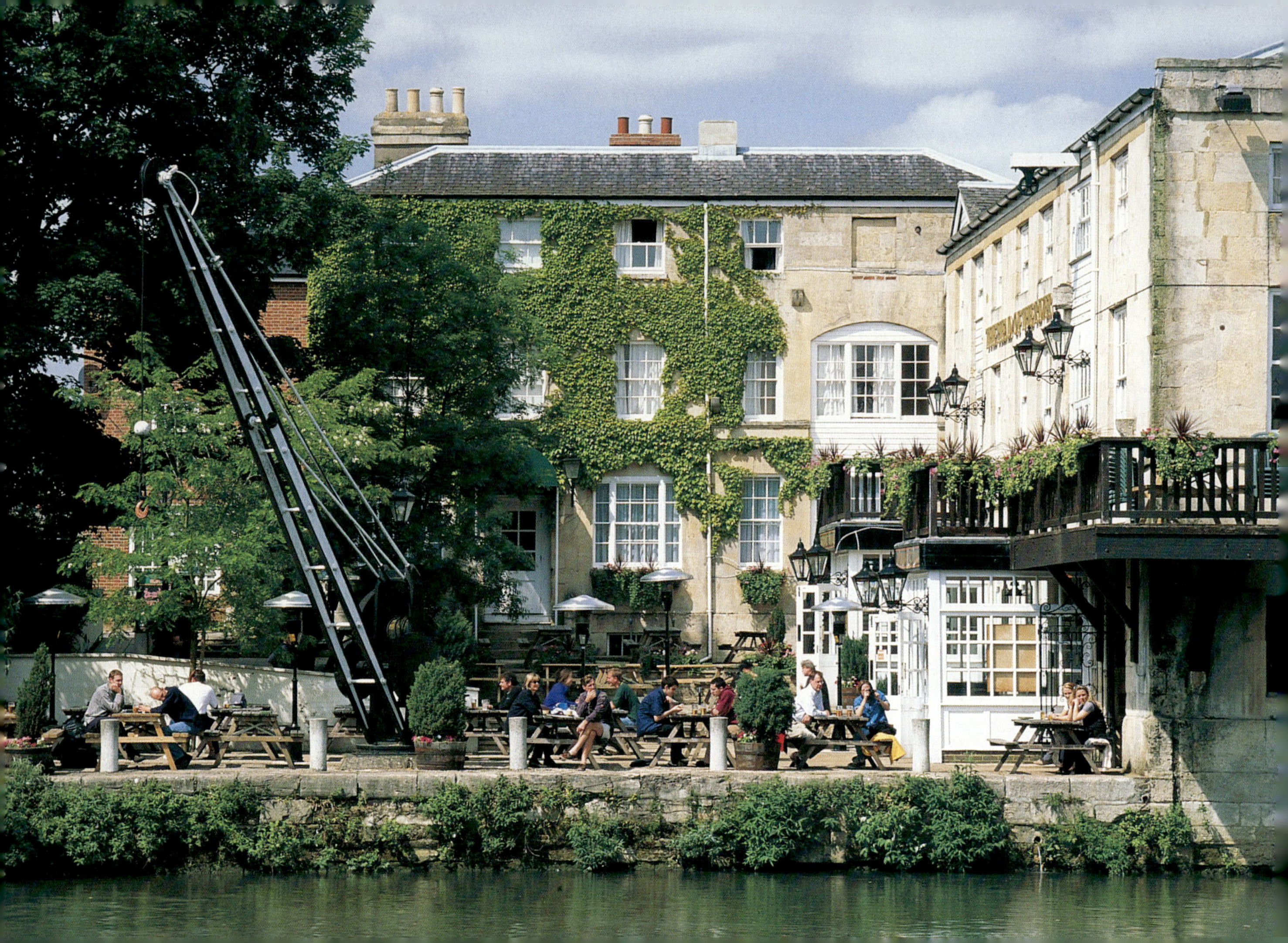

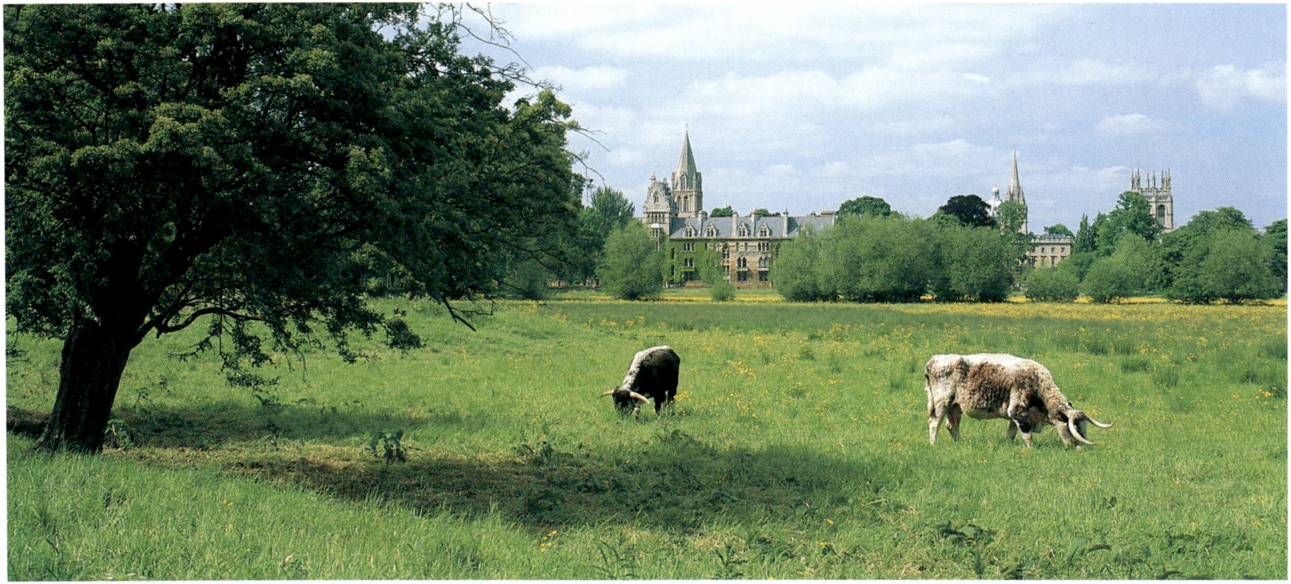

HEAD OF THE RIVER Folly Bridge

Now a very popular pub, the Head of the River was originally a wharf house, built in 1827 for Salter Bros who still operate boats on the River Thames. It was converted to a public house in 1977 and named after the boat races held nearby in Eights Week. The winner at the end of the week is called the 'Head of the River'.

CHRIST CHURCH MEADOW

Spires and towers, and pinnacles, and the great dome of the Radcliffe Library, appeared over the high elms. The banks of Ilyssus, and the groves of Academus, could never have presented a sight more beautiful.

Robert Southey
Letters from England by Don Manuel Alvarez Espriella 1808

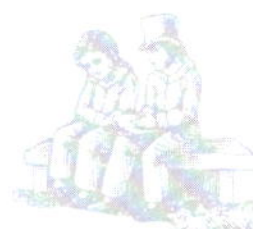

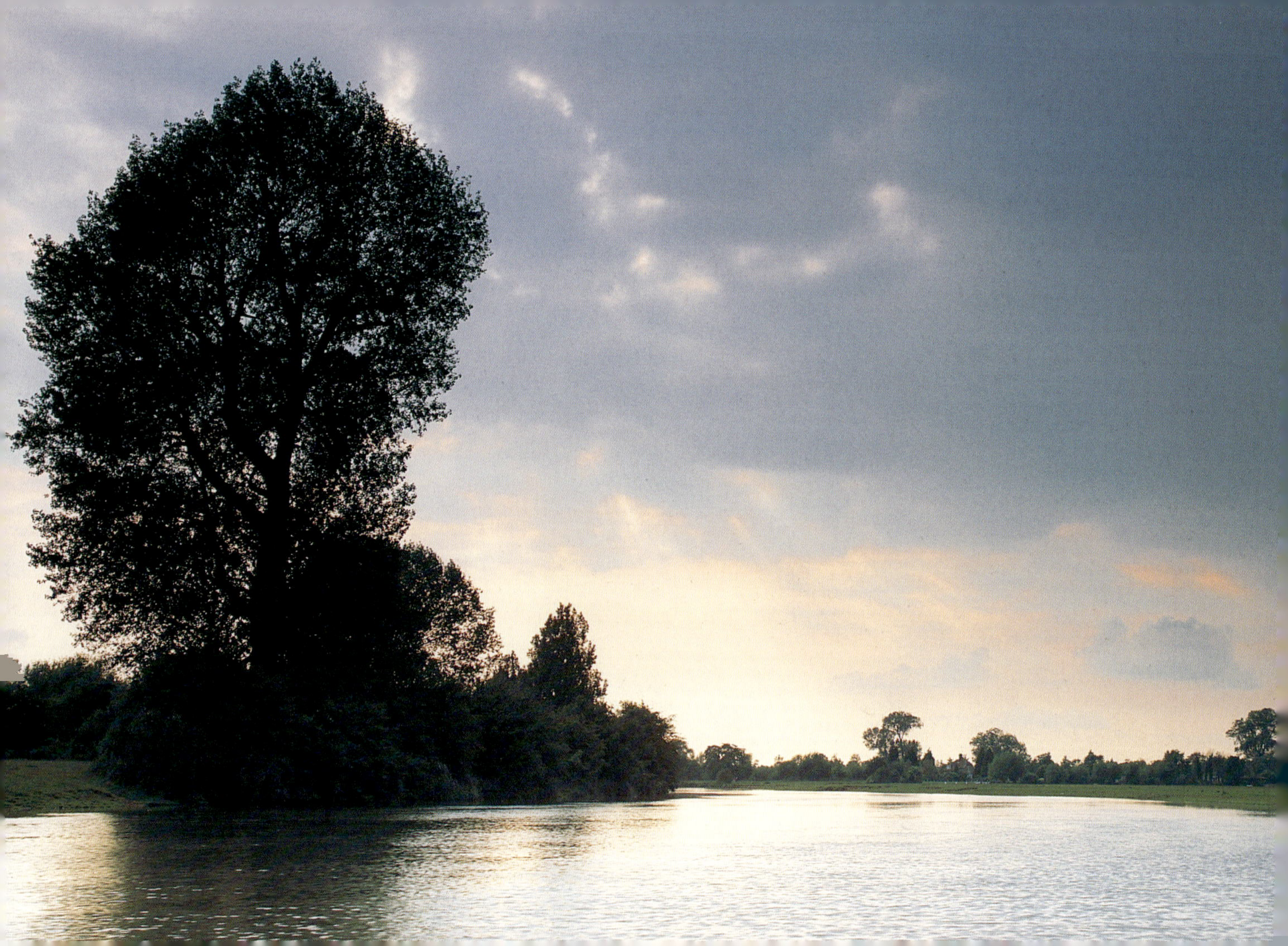

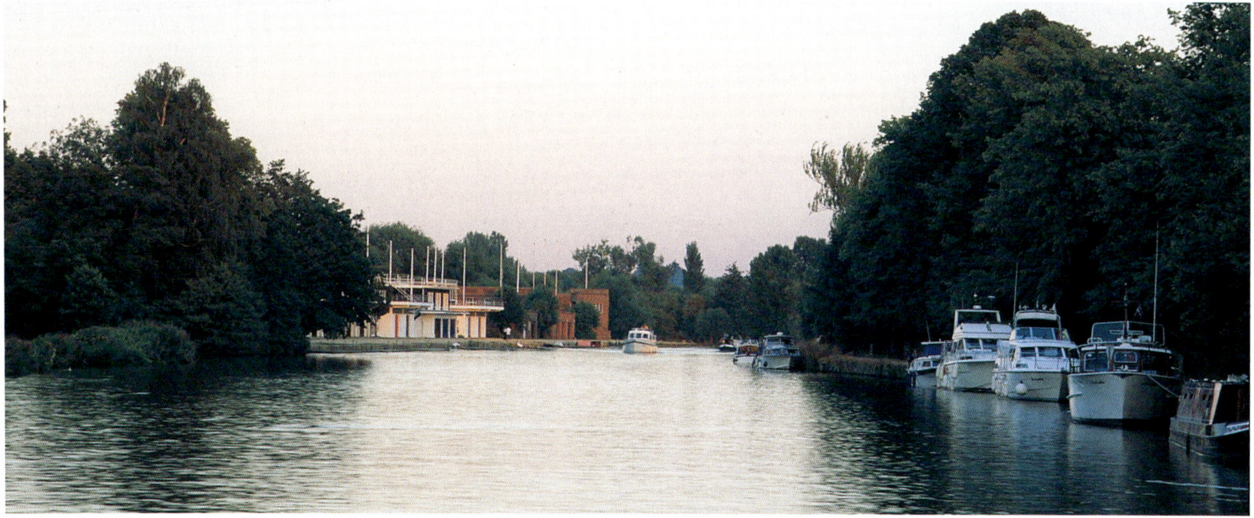

RIVER THAMES
Port Meadow

Long has paled that sunny sky:
Echoes fade and memories die:
Autumn frosts have slain July.

Lewis Carroll
Through the Looking-Glass and What Alice Found There 1871

COLLEGE BOAT HOUSES River Isis

As for the clubs, rowing takes precedence. It may be that a college has not shown a single man in a first class of the schools for years; but if it is top of the river, its position, at any rate socially, is good … it is the centre of life and gaiety during the most beautiful part of the year, the Eights and subsequent weeks … Friends are asked up, and those of the opposite sex are eagerly welcomed. The barges are crowded, white dresses flutter, luncheons are arranged up river, friends are introduced, excursions are arranged, and laughter fills the air.

Norman J. Davidson *Things Seen in Oxford* 1915

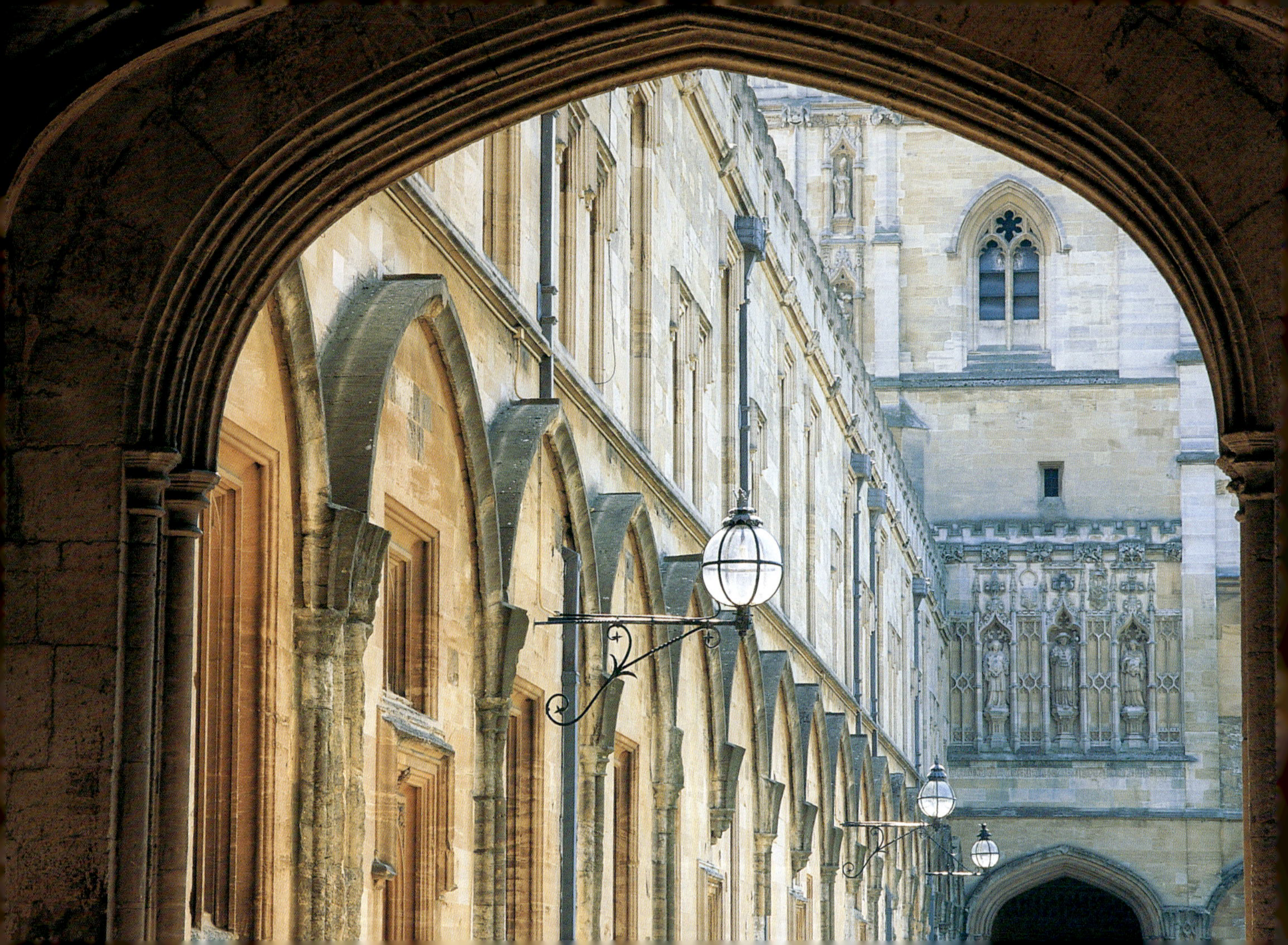

CHRIST CHURCH
Tom Quad

If there had been nothing else in Oxford but this one establishment, my anticipations would not have been disappointed.

Nathaniel Hawthorne
English Notebooks
1856

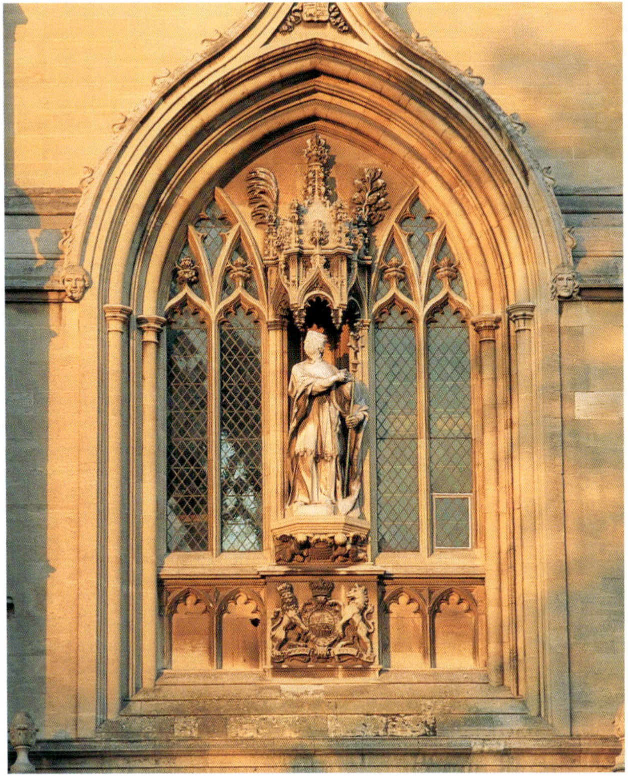

CHRIST CHURCH
Statue of Cardinal Wolsey, Tom Tower

Wolsey ... determined to erect a college where the new learning, which then at its prosperous flood was pouring over Europe, should be cultivated in the service of the old Church. He determined that his college should be erected on a scale so magnificent and vast that no other foundation in Europe could be put in comparison with it. The name of the college was to be Cardinal College.

Frederick Arnold
Oxford and Cambridge: Their Memories and Associations
1873

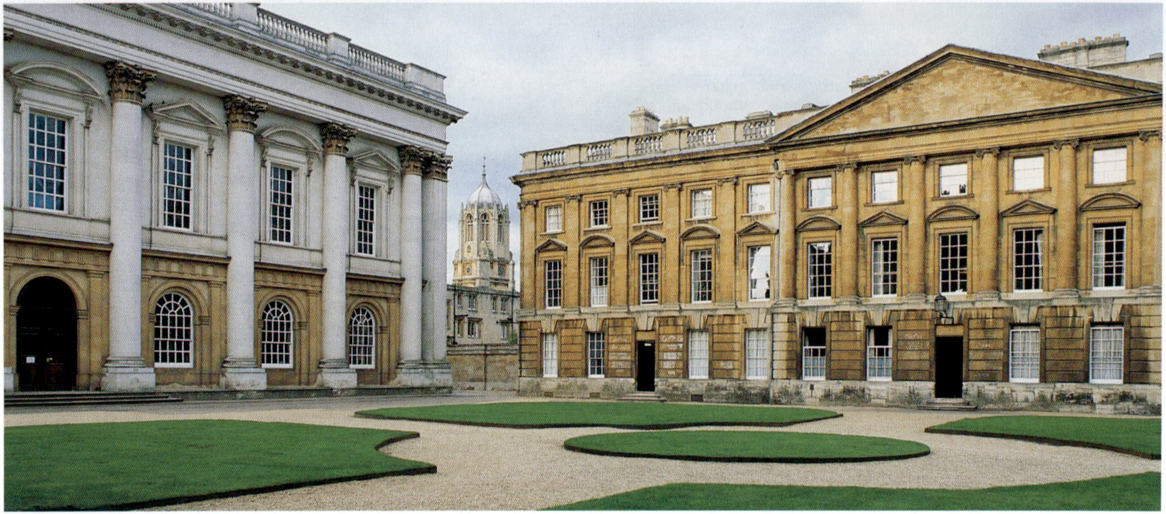

CHRIST CHURCH Peckwater Quad

It was here that William Penn, who, having entered the University during the Protectorate, was provoked by the restoration of the ancient ceremonial, flew with his associates upon the Christ Church students when they appeared for the first time in their white surplices, and tore the hated garments to pieces.

A Handbook for Travellers in Berks, Bucks and Oxfordshire 1860

CHRIST CHURCH Hall

… the fellows or dons as they call them in Oxford … are seated at a table on a platform at the extreme end of the large hall. Dinner being finished, the student, five times out of six, spends his evening at some 'wine', that is he joins his friends in their rooms or they come to him to drink port and sherry, smoke a pipe or a cigar, have some music or a game of cards …

Paul Bourget *Some Impressions of Oxford* 1901

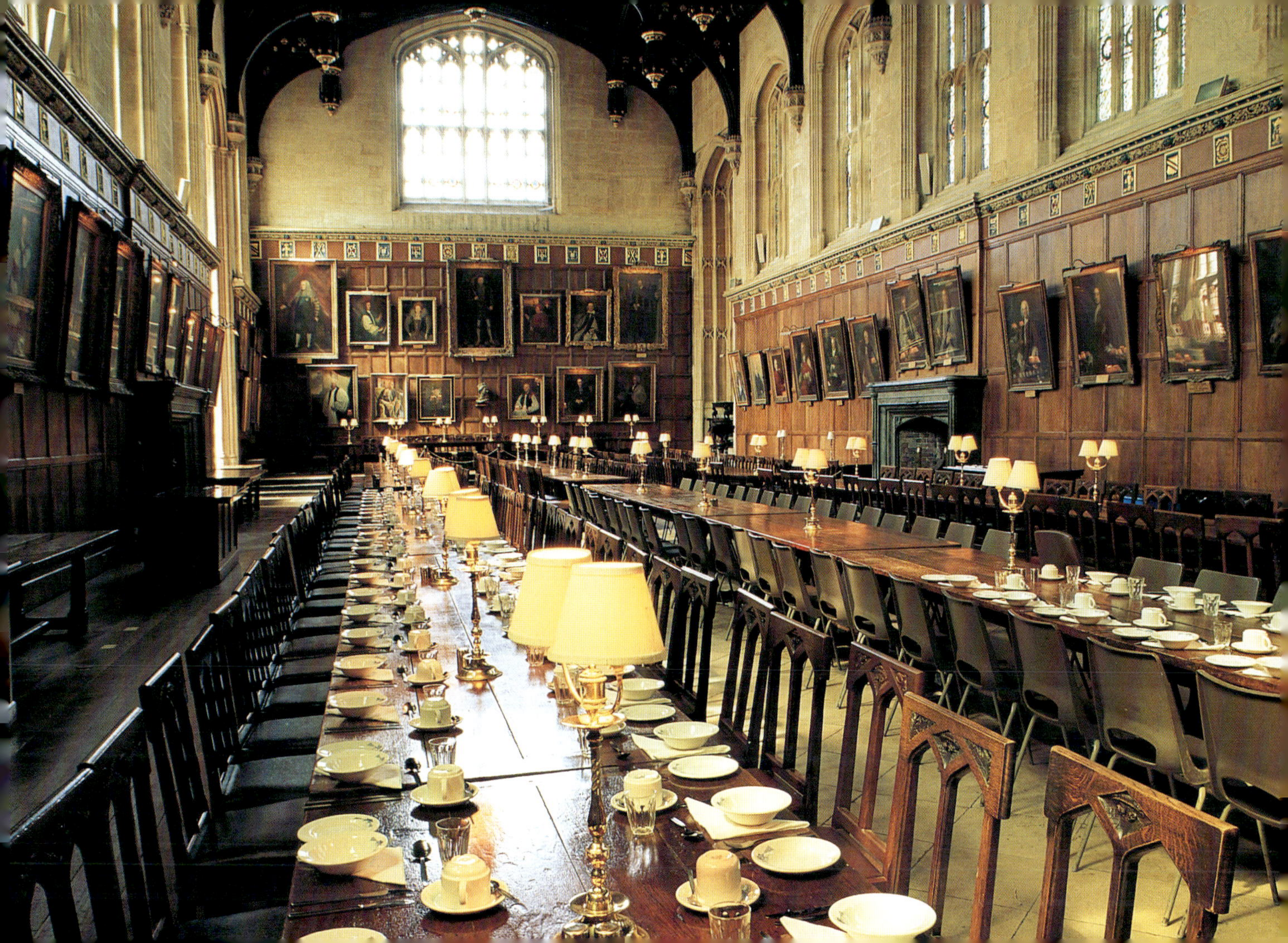

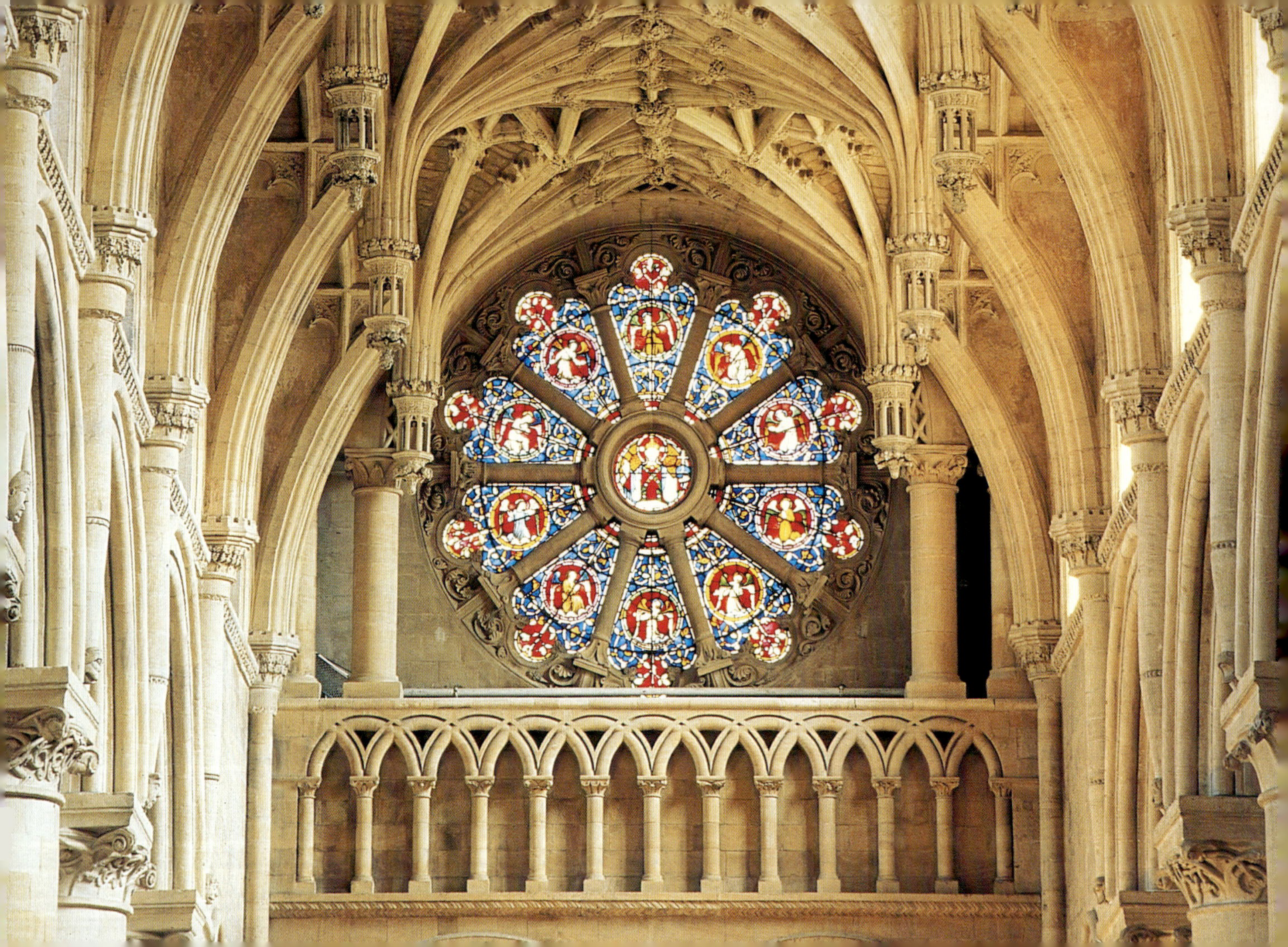

CHRIST CHURCH CATHEDRAL

After the fall of Cardinal Wolsey the college was re-founded by Henry VIII as Christ Church, its Latin name, Aedes Christi, giving it the informal name of 'The House'. Its chapel had formerly been the church of a priory of Augustinian Canons and Wolsey had intended to rebuild it on the same scale as his college. However, the king had other ideas and, uniquely, the college chapel also became the cathedral of the new diocese of Oxford.

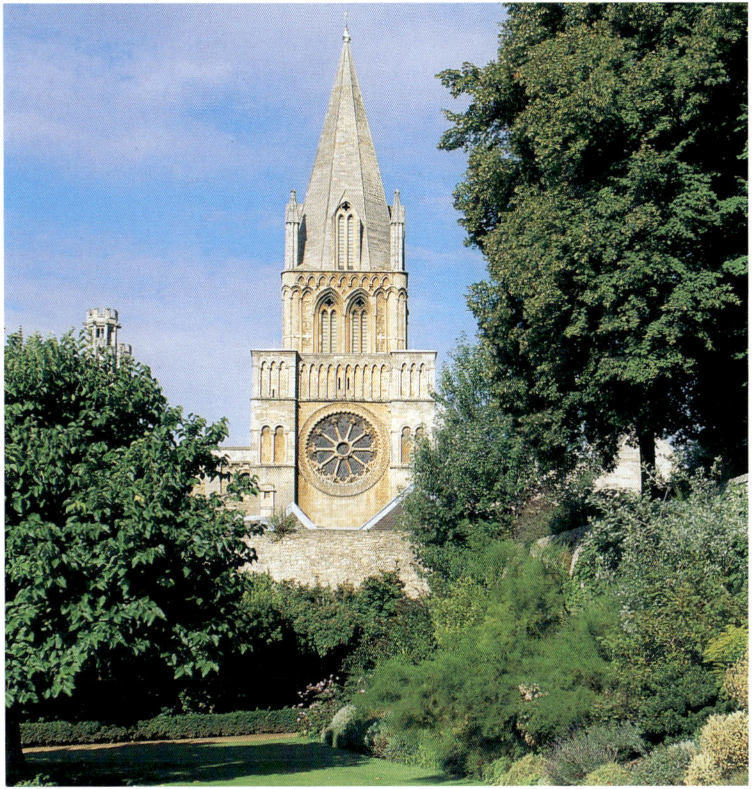

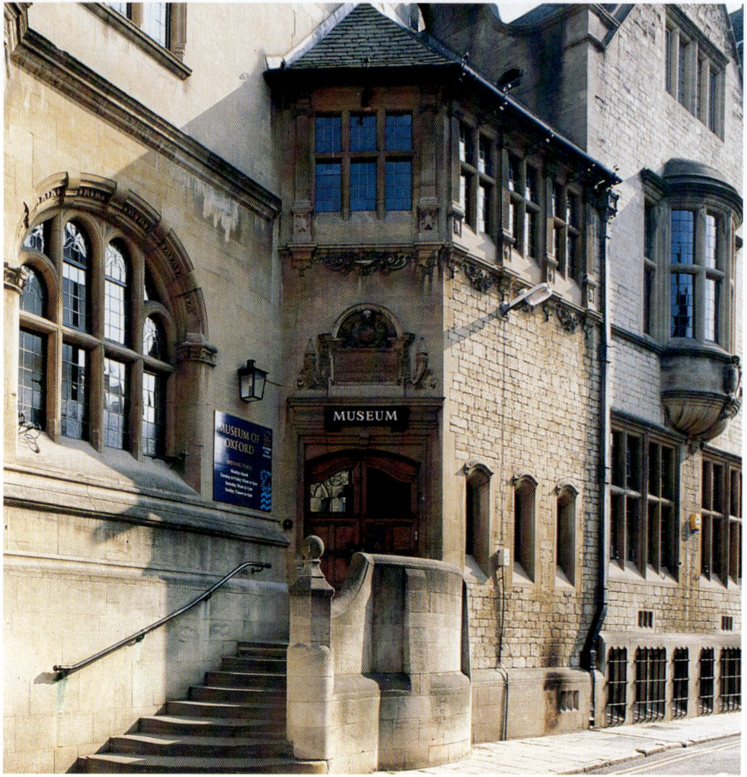

MUSEUM OF OXFORD
St Aldates

New municipal buildings, town hall, offices and public library, were opened by the then Prince of Wales in 1897. The architecture of the public library was more vernacular than for the rest of the building and shows the influence of the Arts and Crafts Movement. The library moved to Westgate in 1978 and the building became the Museum of Oxford.

ORIEL STREET

… they descended into the High Street, walking all abreast, the two ladies together, with a gentlemen on either flank. This formation answered well enough in High Street … But when they had wheeled into Oriel Lane the narrow pavement at once threw the line into confusion, and after one or two fruitless attempts to take up the dressing they settled down into the more natural formation of close column of couples …

Thomas Hughes *Tom Brown at Oxford* 1861

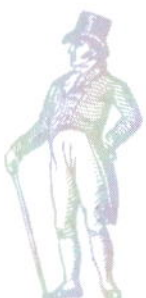

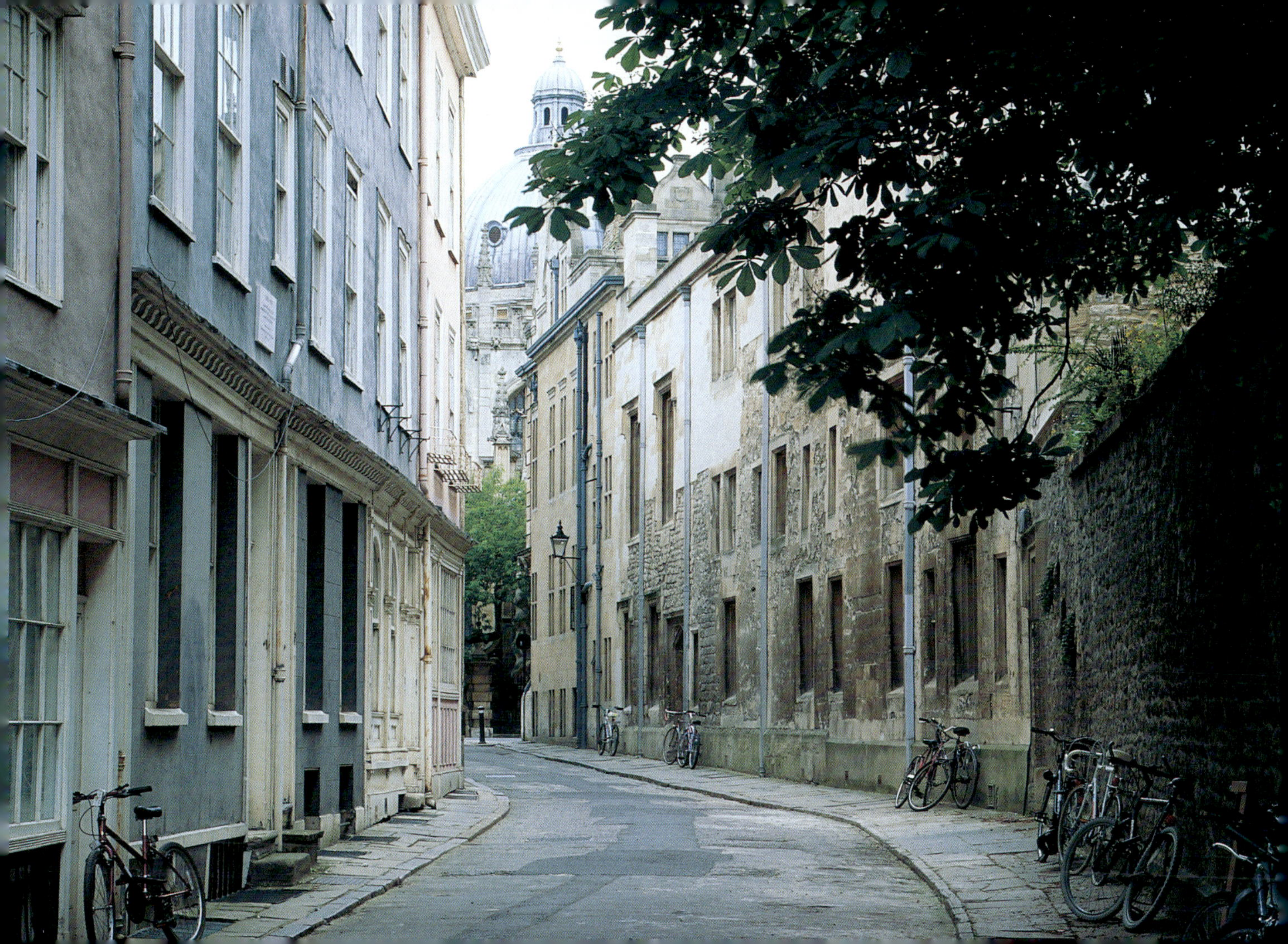

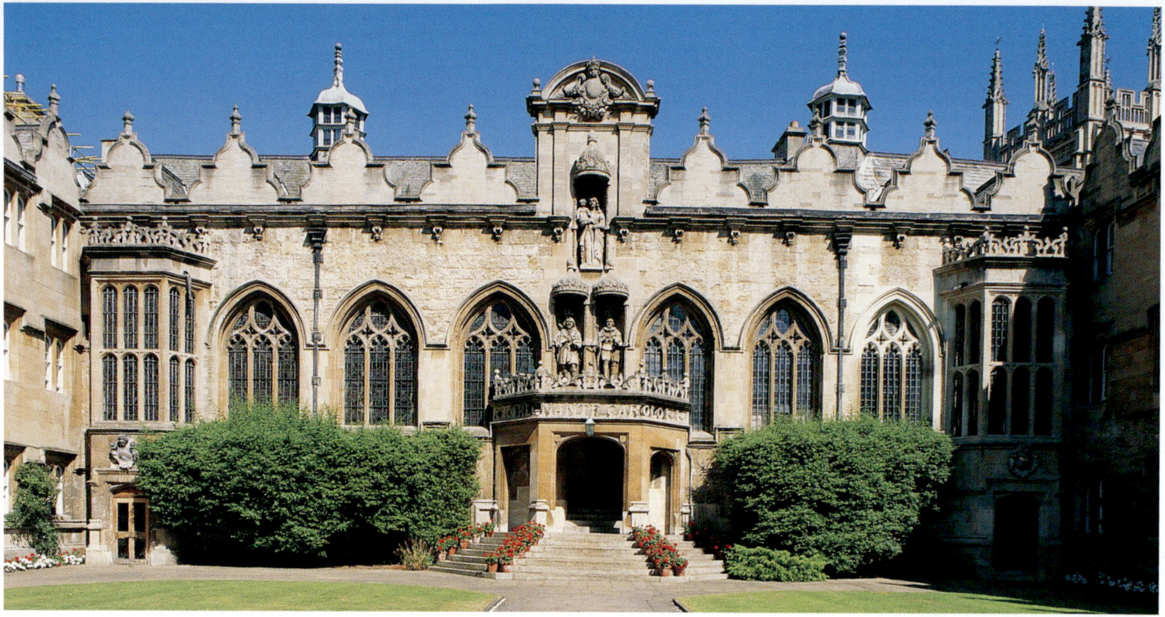

ORIEL COLLEGE Front Quad

In 1752 Gilbert White of Selborne was Proctor … When he treated the Masters of Arts in Oriel Hall they ate a hundred pounds weight of biscuits – not, we trust, without marmalade.

Andrew Lang *Oxford* 1882

MERTON STREET

They wandered at random, choosing the narrower ways and coming suddenly on colleges and long old walls. Nothing seemed modern now. The past had them by the throat.

John Galsworthy *The End of the Chapter* 1935

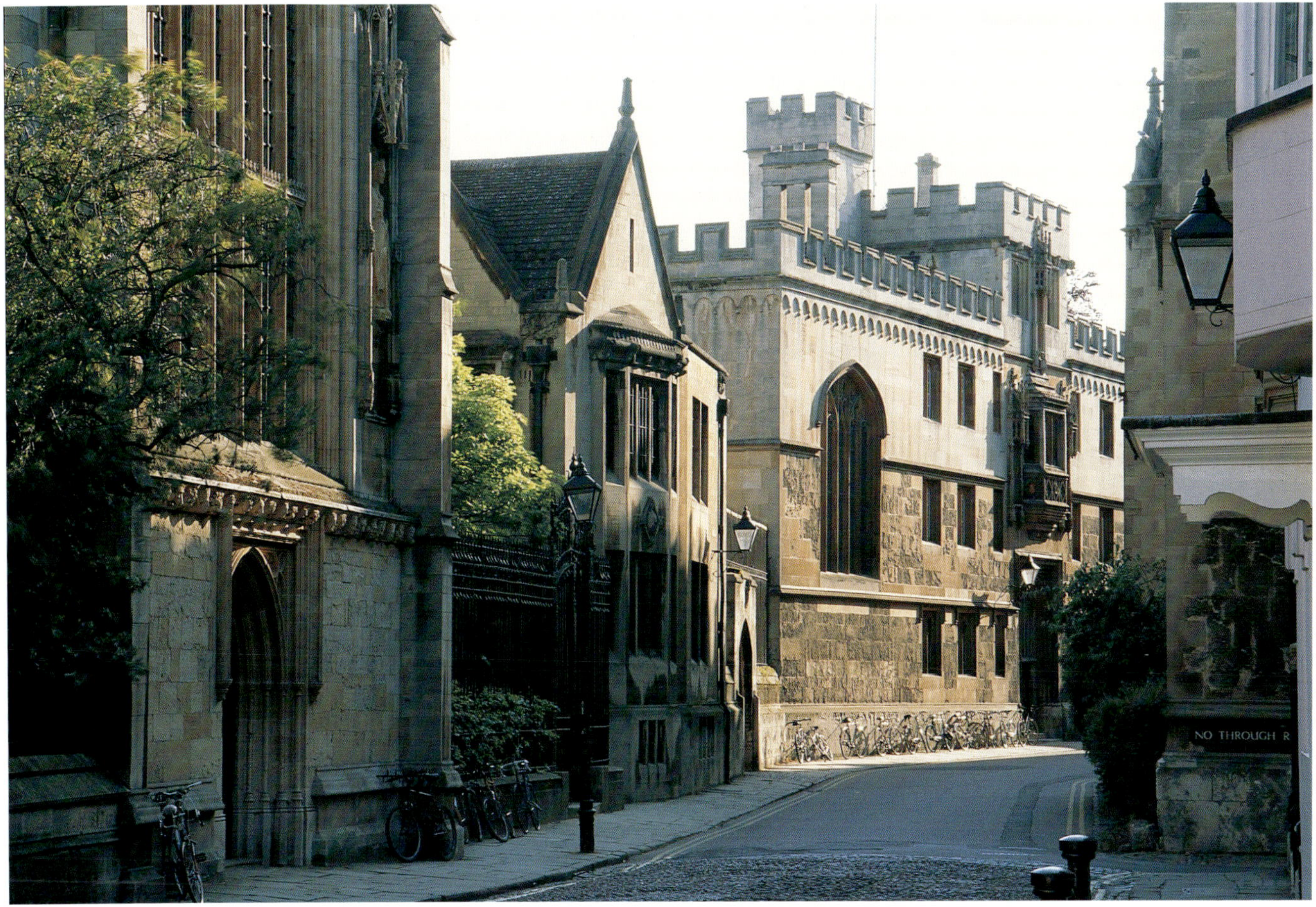
NO THROUGH R

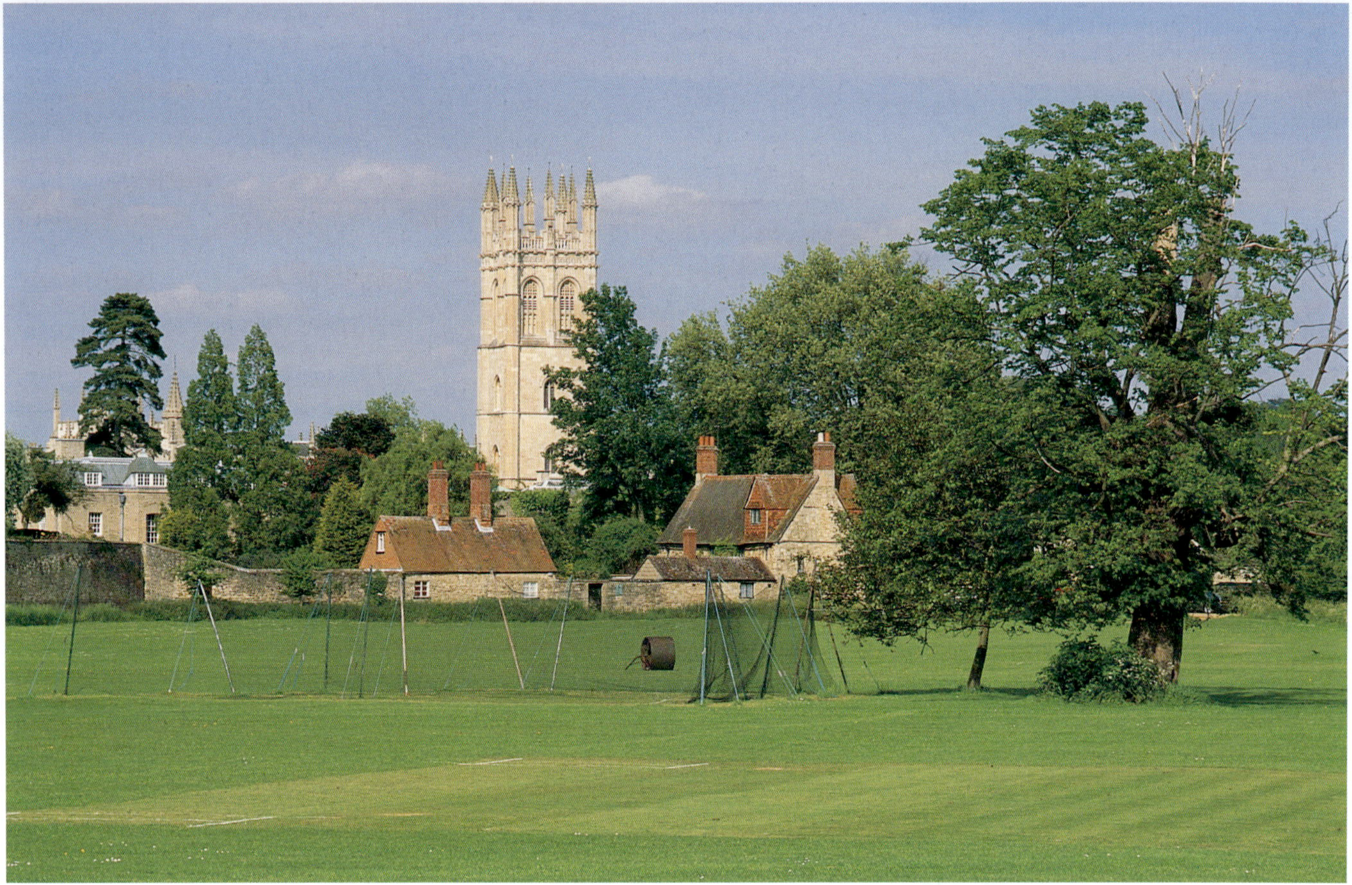

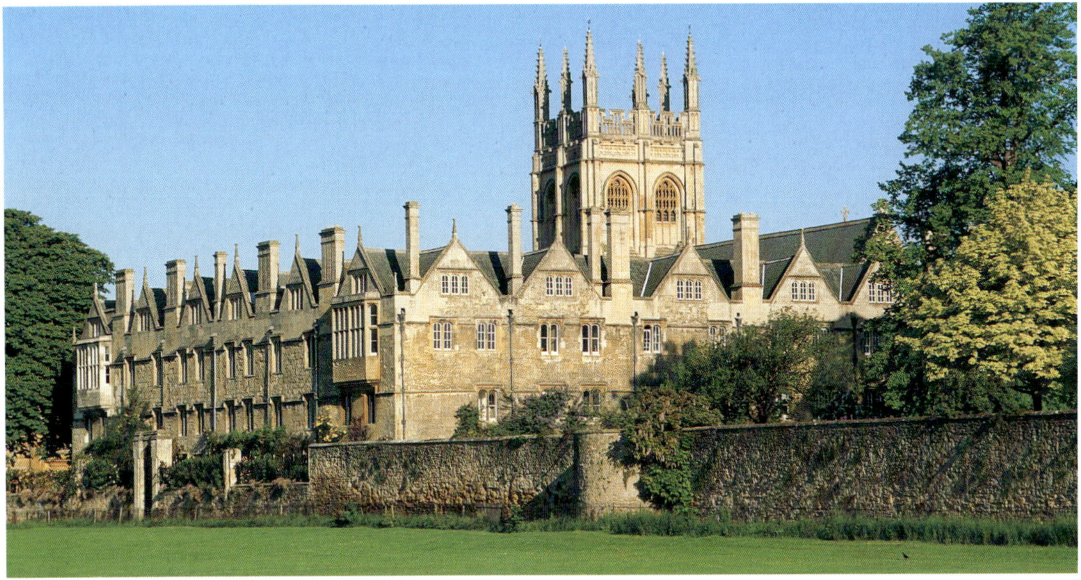

MERTON FIELDS

I directed my steps towards Magdalen Tower, rising gracefully from behind a tall tree in the centre of the field … A perfect country scene, I thought, with an ancient city for background, and sunshine and shadow chasing each other over the fields and among the trees.

CHIANG YEE *The Silent Traveller in Oxford* 1946

MERTON COLLEGE

In medieval times Jews could not be buried within the city walls. It is said that they took their dead along a path running outside the walls to their cemetery near Magdalen Bridge. The path, which still runs in front of a surviving stretch of the old city wall beneath Merton College, is known as Dead Man's Walk.

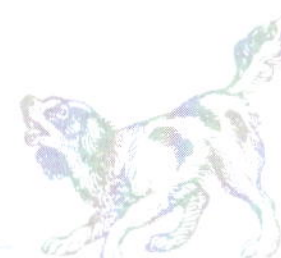

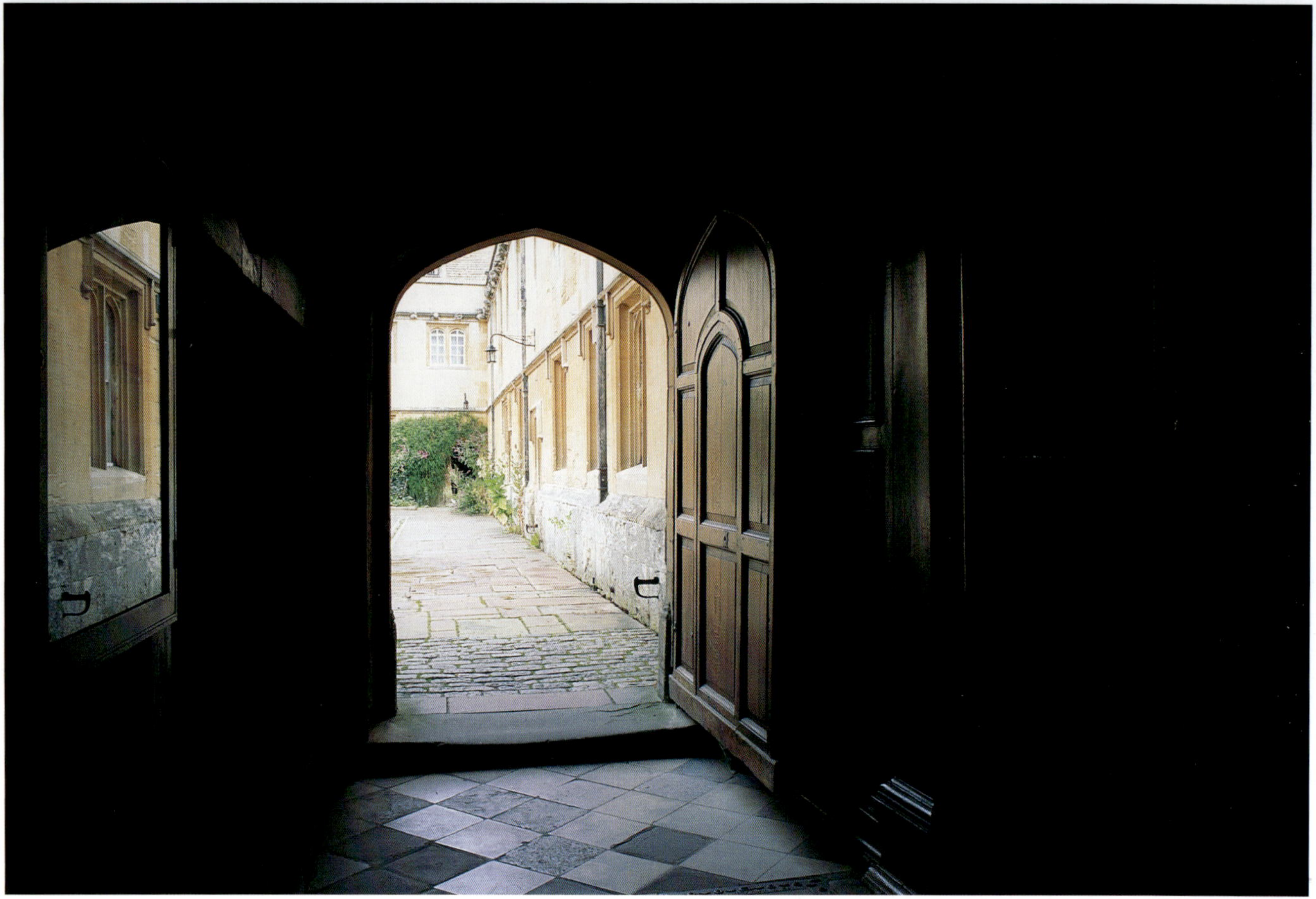

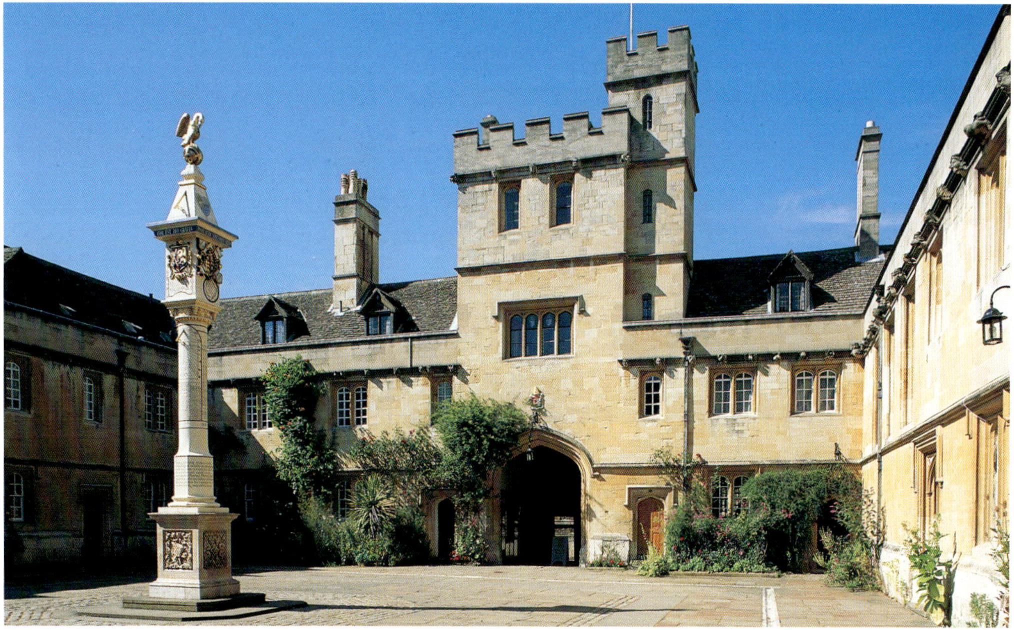

CORPUS CHRISTI COLLEGE Front Quad

The sundial is surmounted by the emblem of the college, a pelican pecking at her own breast to feed her young – a symbol of the Eucharist. Around the plinth is a perpetual calendar.

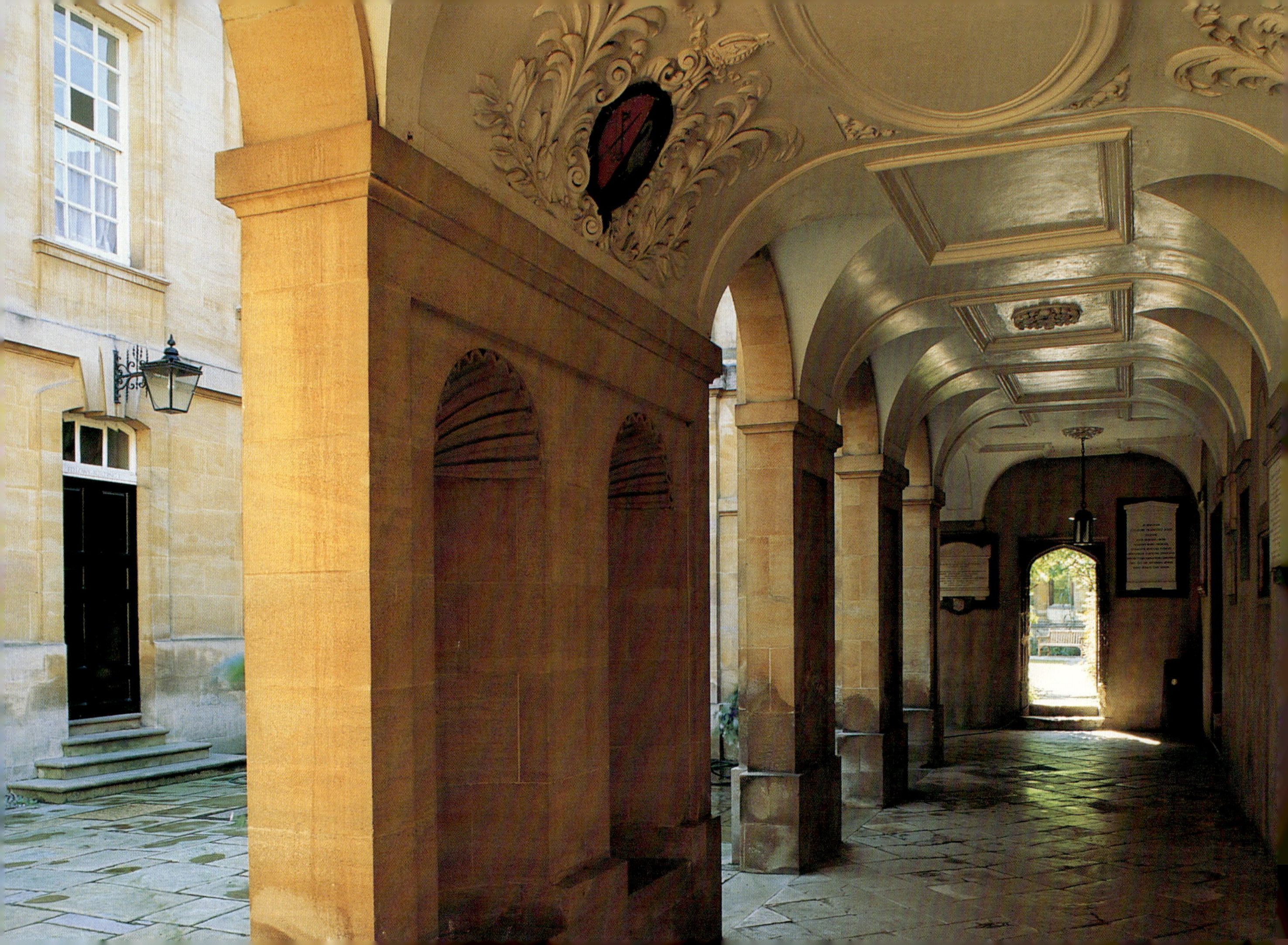

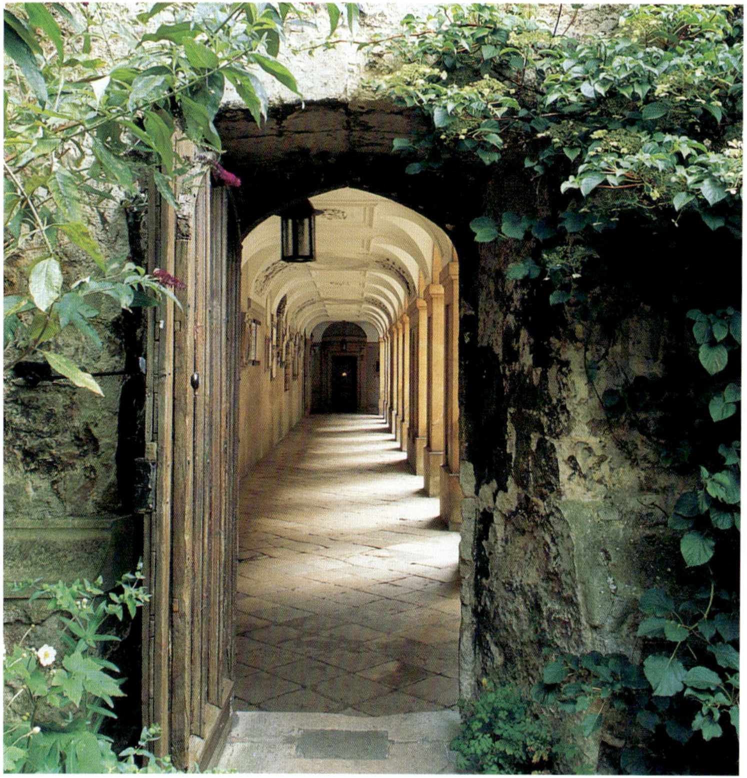

CORPUS CHRISTI COLLEGE
Fellows' Quad – Cloister

Ye know, in this our quiet spot have lived
   Hearts close united by affection's tie,
Wit that might shine in Courts as well as Quads,
   And social virtues with which few can vie.

Thomas Fausset
From a letter, written to an absentee comrade
at the close of term
1907

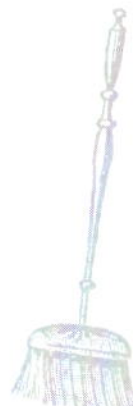

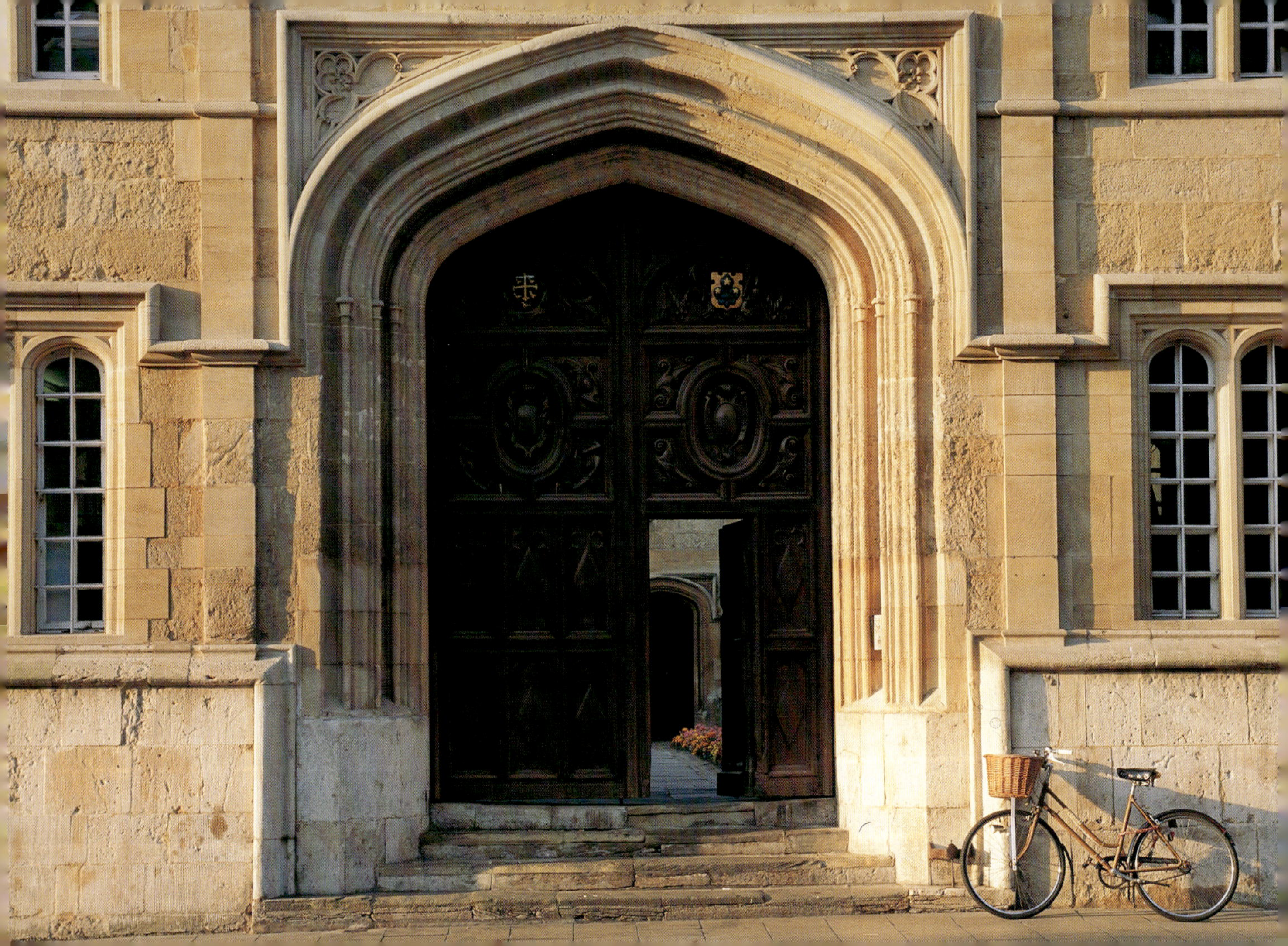

UNIVERSITY COLLEGE

… at night heavy wooden gates are closed upon the street, barred with iron, locked with elaborate padlocks, pierced only by a small postern and powerfully suggesting chain-mail and boiling oil.

Behind these defences, though, all is delightful intimacy.

JAN MORRIS
Oxford
1965

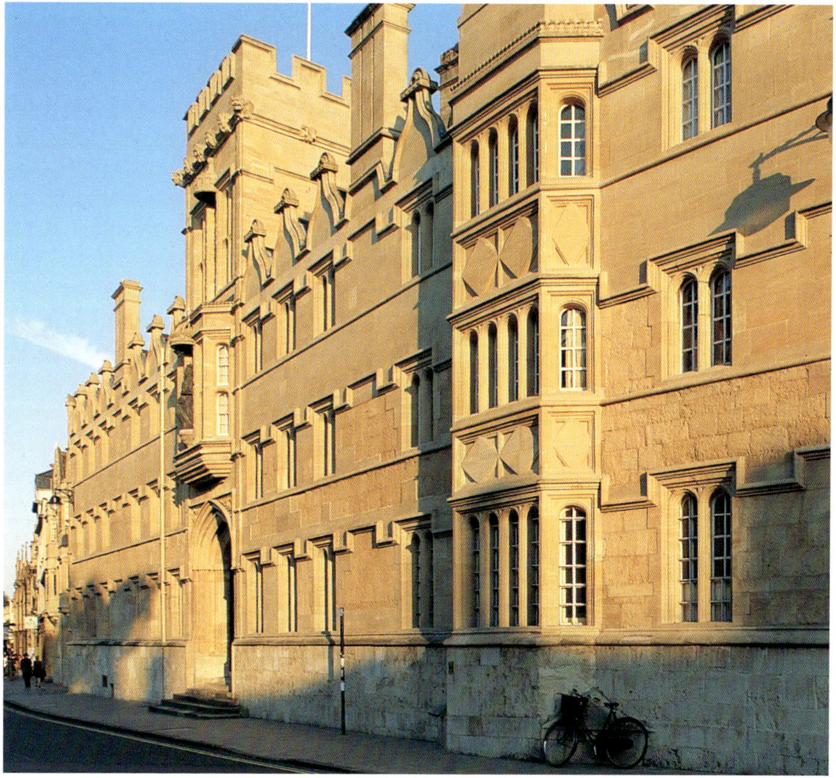

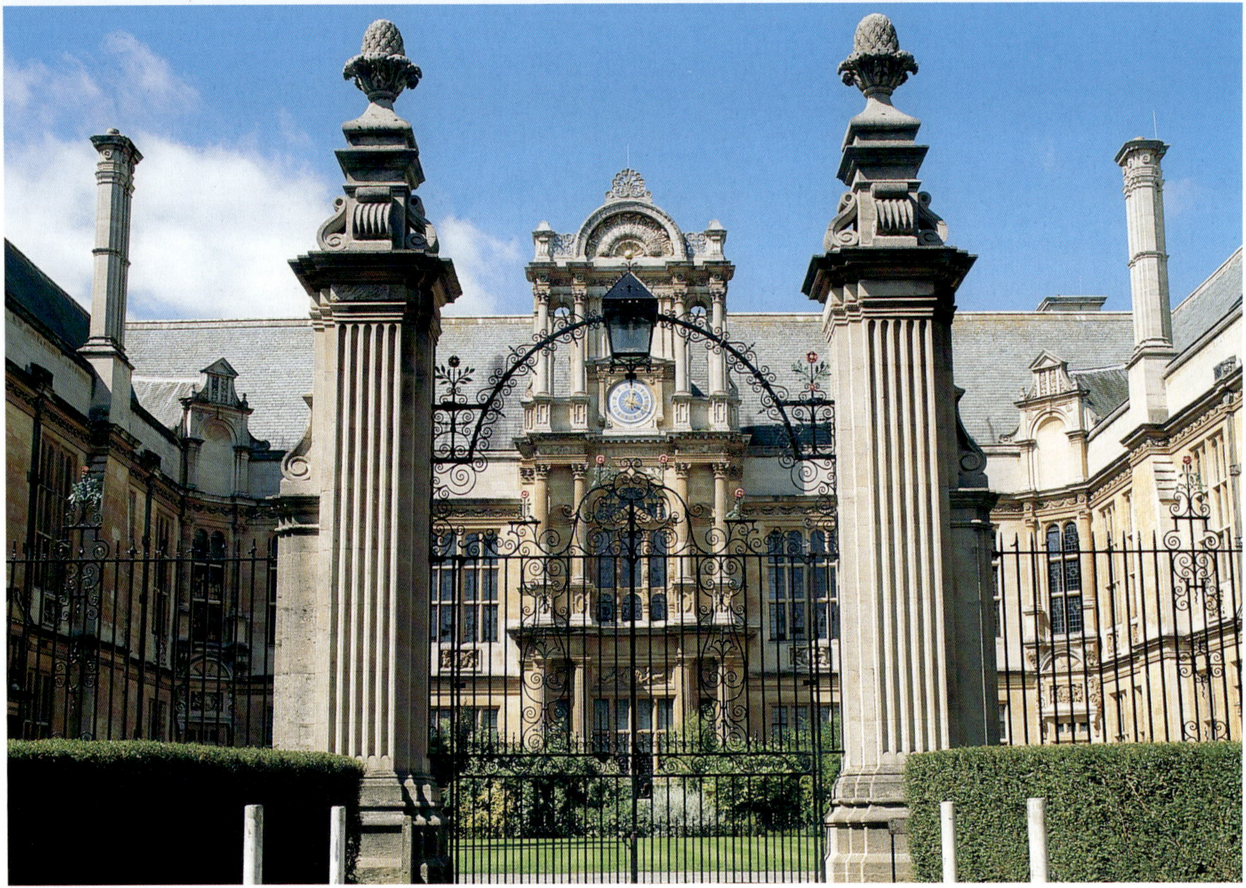

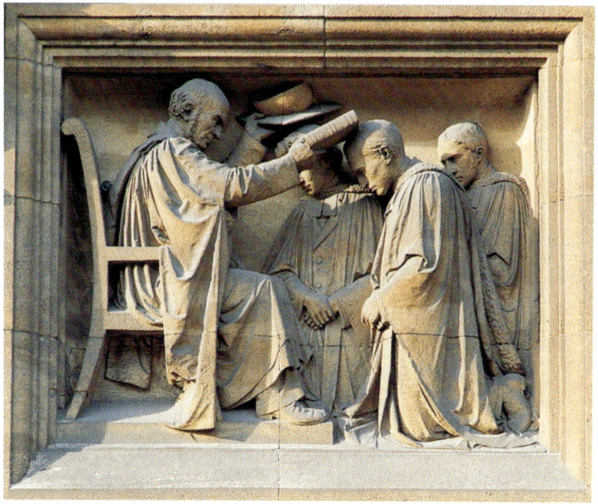 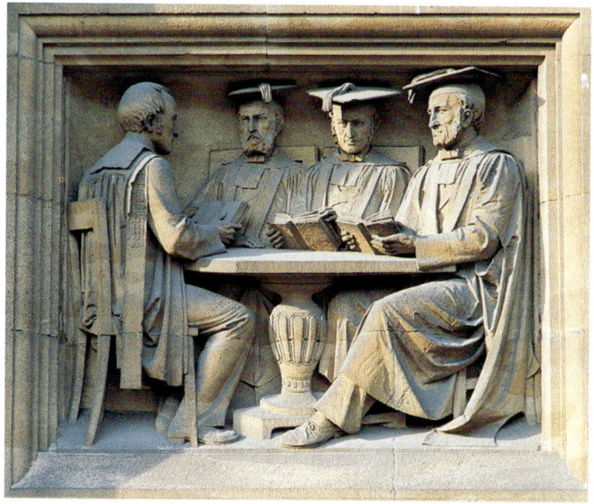

EXAMINATION SCHOOLS Merton Street

… a place which few Oxford men have entered save under compulsion, and of which when entered, they have never studied the artistic merits …

L. Rice-Oxley *Oxford Renowned* 1925

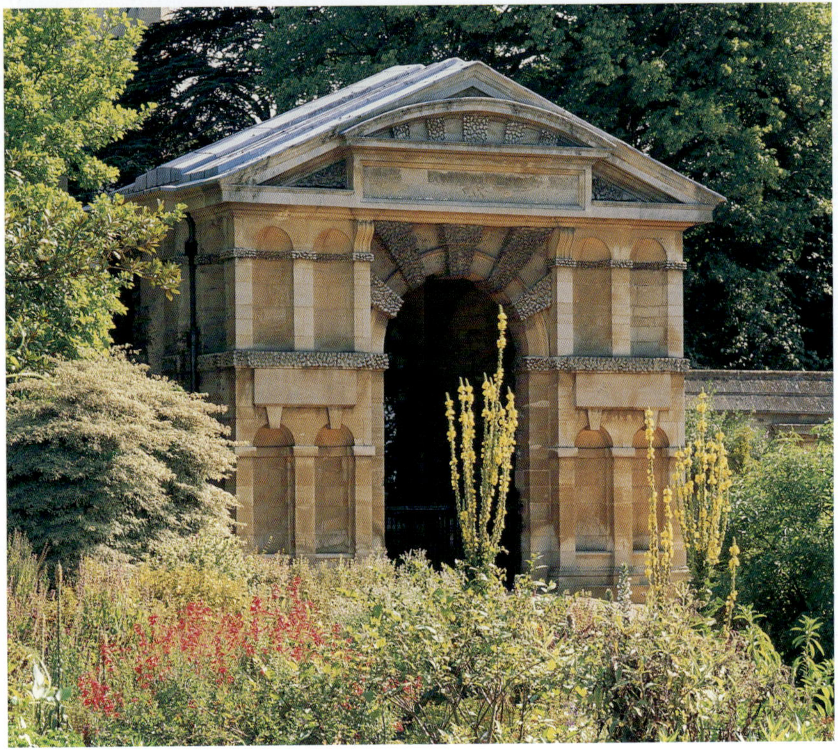

BOTANIC GARDEN
High Street

The Oxford Botanical Garden, behind high walls opposite Magdalen, is the oldest in Great Britain: and what with its crumbled stones and shaded benches, its urns and pots and greenhouses, the Cherwell flowing sweetly beside its lawns and the goldfish who twitch in its ornamental pond – with the great tower of Magdalen serene above its gate, and the spires peering always between its foliage, there can be few better places in England for the contemplation of flowers.

Jan Morris
Oxford
1965

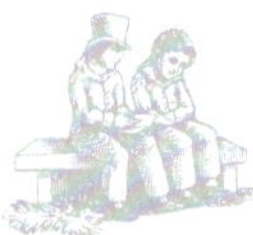

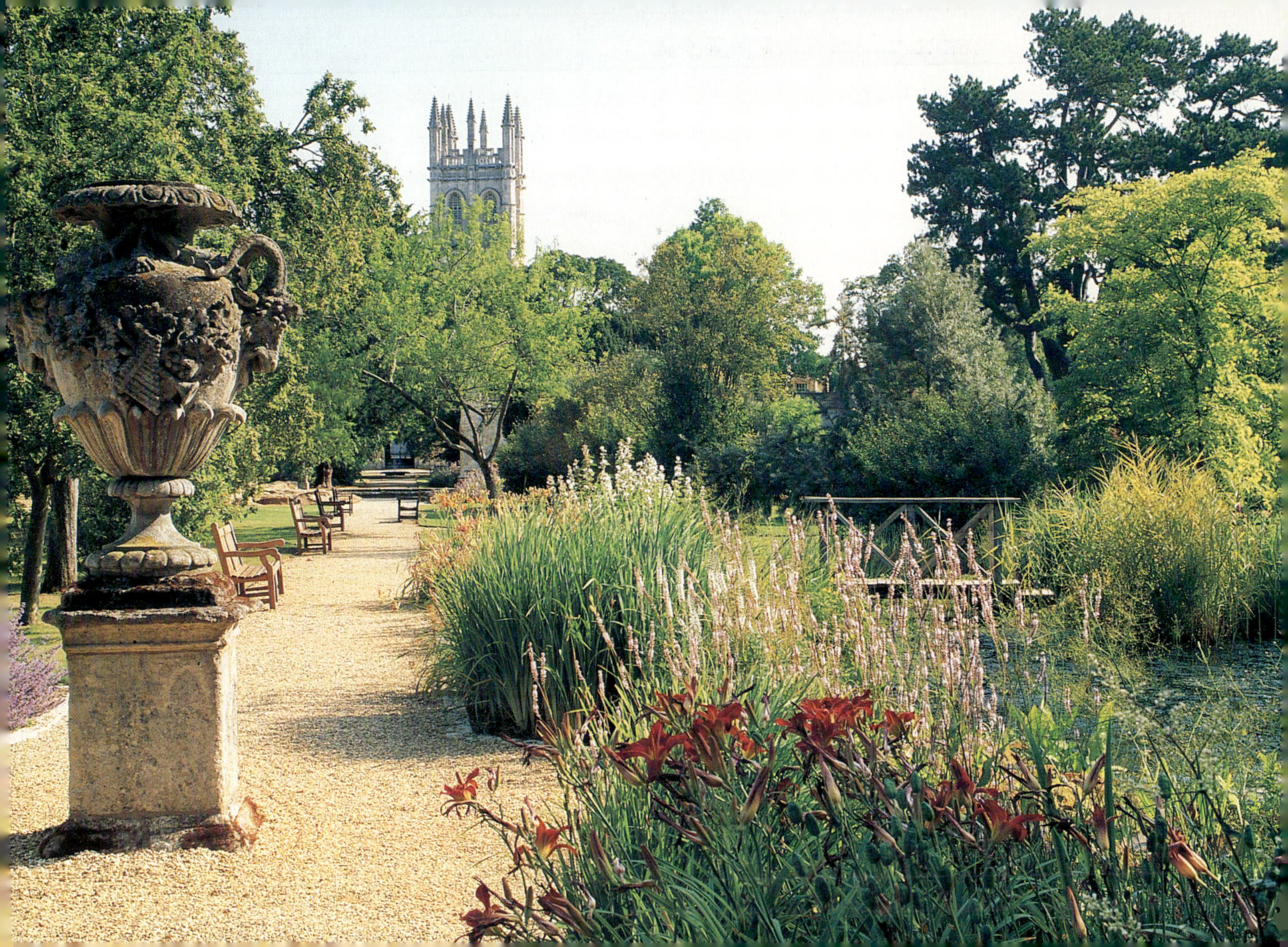

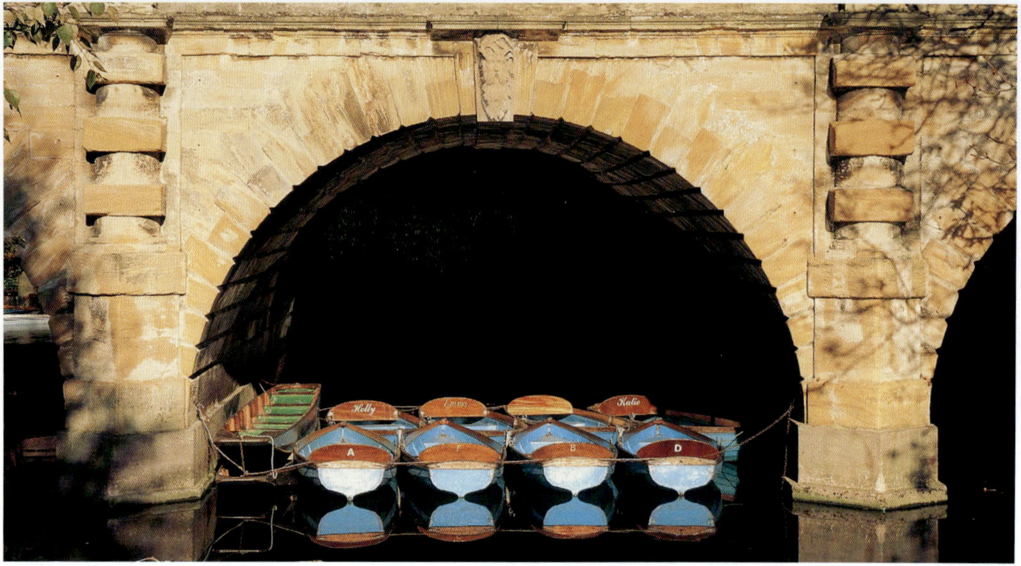

MAGDALEN BRIDGE

If it were not the paradise that man has made it Oxford would be beautiful, for it lies among the meadows at the meeting of the Cherwell and the Isis …

ARTHUR MEE *The King's England – Oxfordshire* 1949

RIVER CHERWELL NEAR MAGDALEN BRIDGE

I … had noticed a number of fish near Magdalen Bridge and I thought how true and right Lao-tzu had been when he said: 'The highest good is like that of water. The goodness of water is that it benefits the ten thousand creatures yet itself does not grumble.'

CHIANG YEE *The Silent Traveller in Oxford* 1946

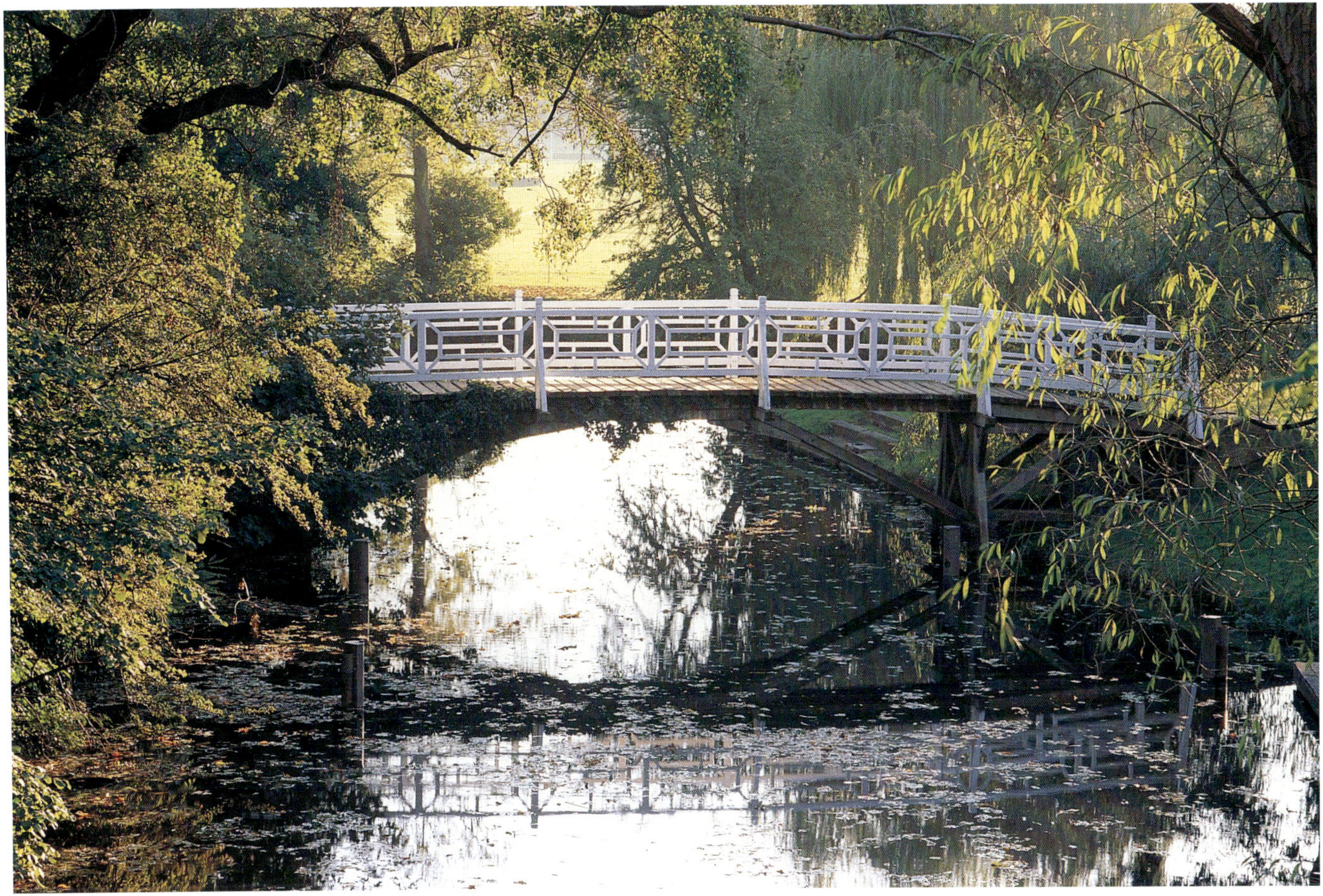

ST MARY'S CHURCH
IFFLEY

The one great attraction to the judicious visitor to the village of Iffley is the Church, one of the most interesting in England …

WARD LOCK
Pictorial and Descriptive Guide to Oxford
1894

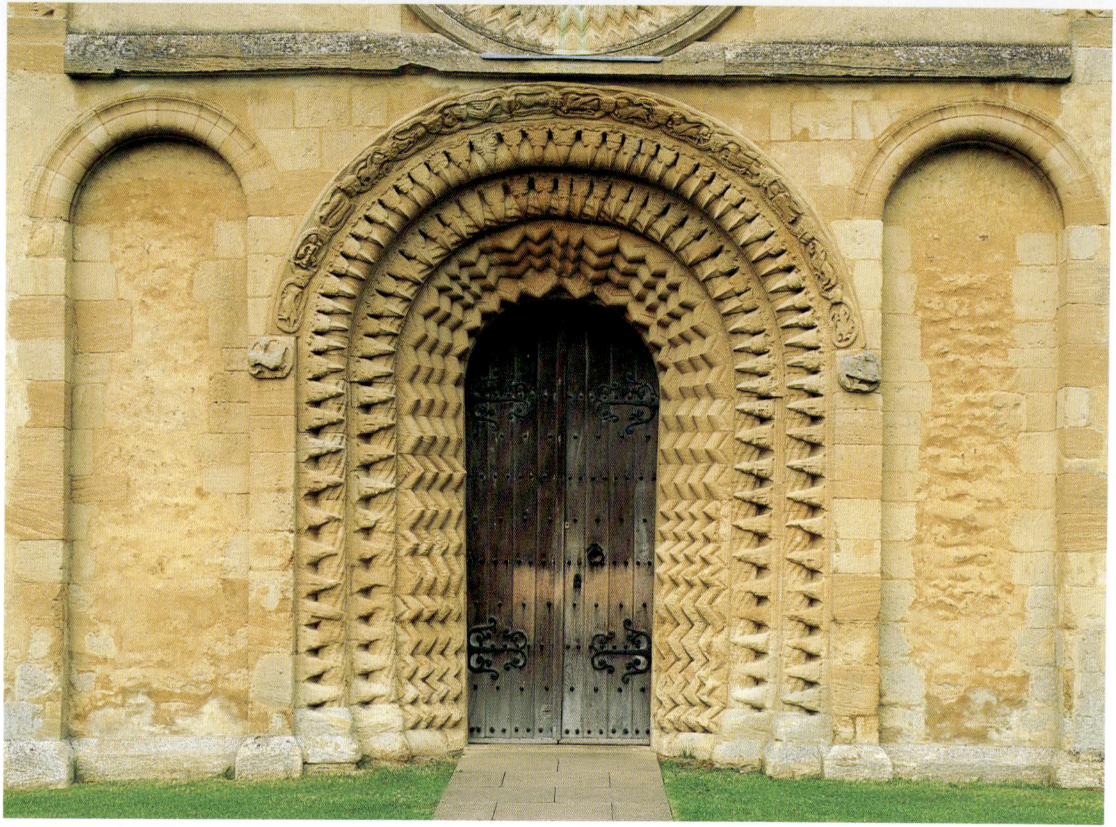

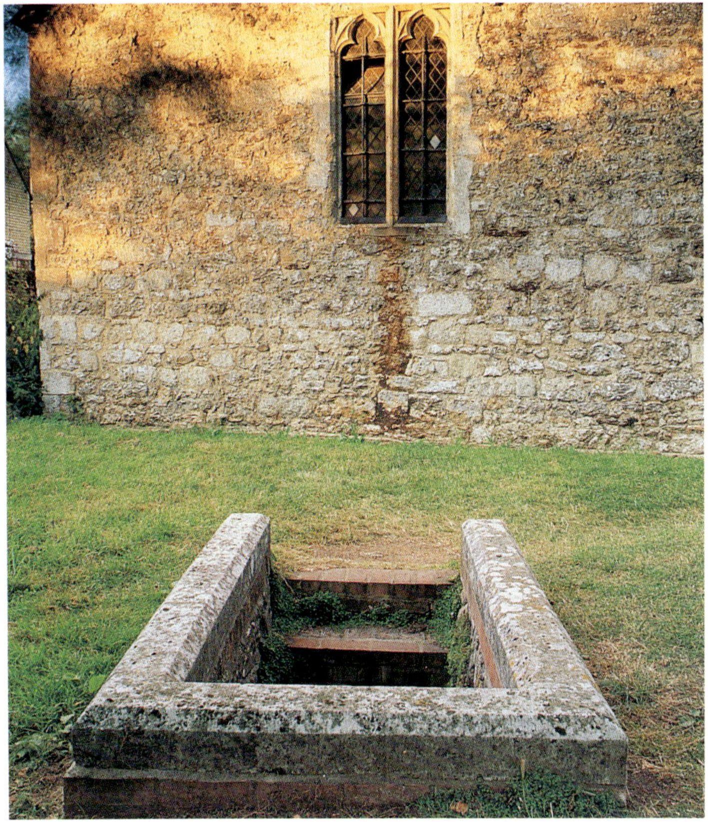

ST MARGARET'S WELL BINSEY

'Once upon a time there were three little sisters,' the Dormouse began … 'and they lived at the bottom of a well –'

'What did they live on?' said Alice, who always took a great interest in questions of eating and drinking.

'They lived on treacle,' said the Dormouse, after thinking a minute or two …

'Why did they live at the bottom of a well?'

The Dormouse again took a minute or two to think about it, and then said, 'It was a treacle-well.'

LEWIS CARROLL
Alice's Adventures in Wonderland
1865

St Margaret's Well in Binsey churchyard is reputed to be the origin of the treacle-well in the story told by the Dormouse.

OXFORD
from Boars Hill

Yet I have seen no place, by inland brook,
Hill-top, or plain, or trim arcaded bowers,
That carries age so nobly in its look,
As Oxford with the sun upon her towers.

F. W. Faber
From 'Aged Cities'
1908

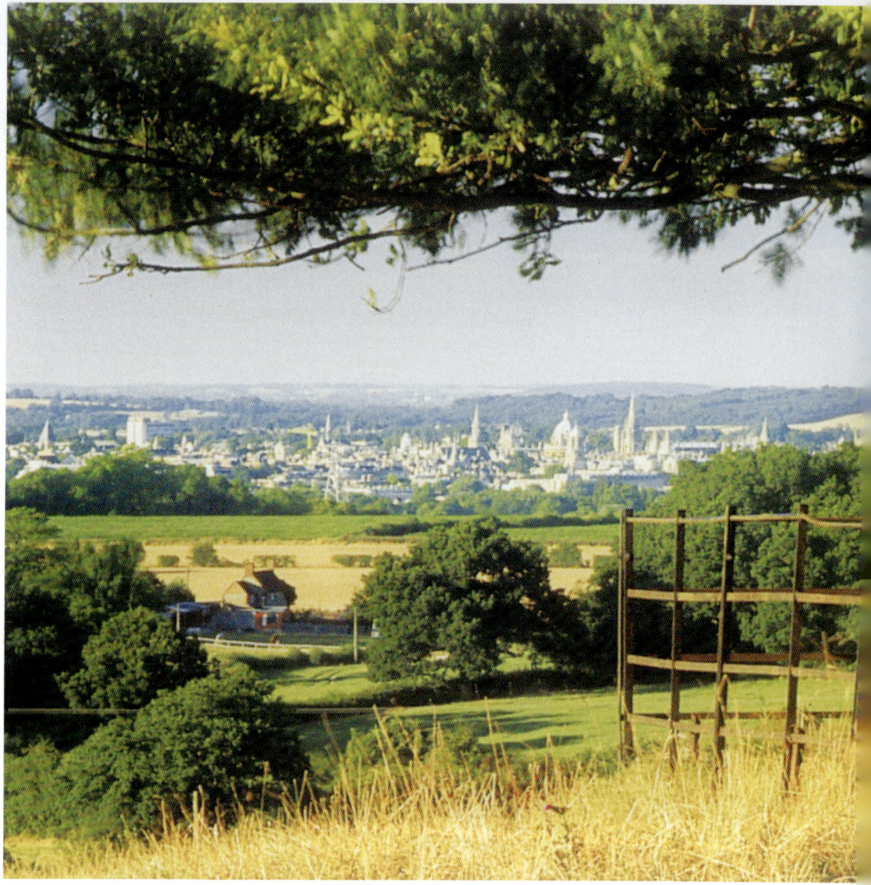

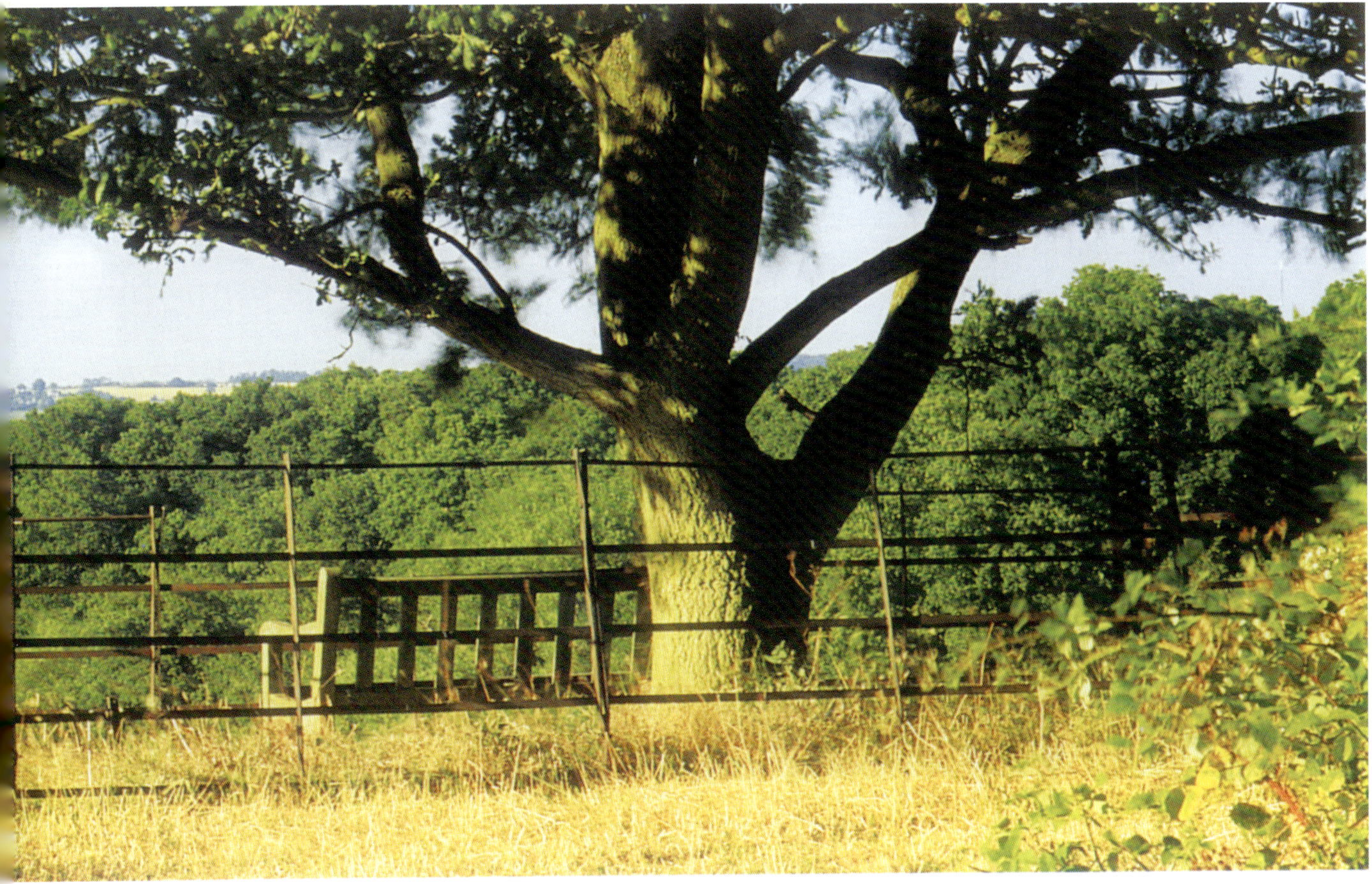

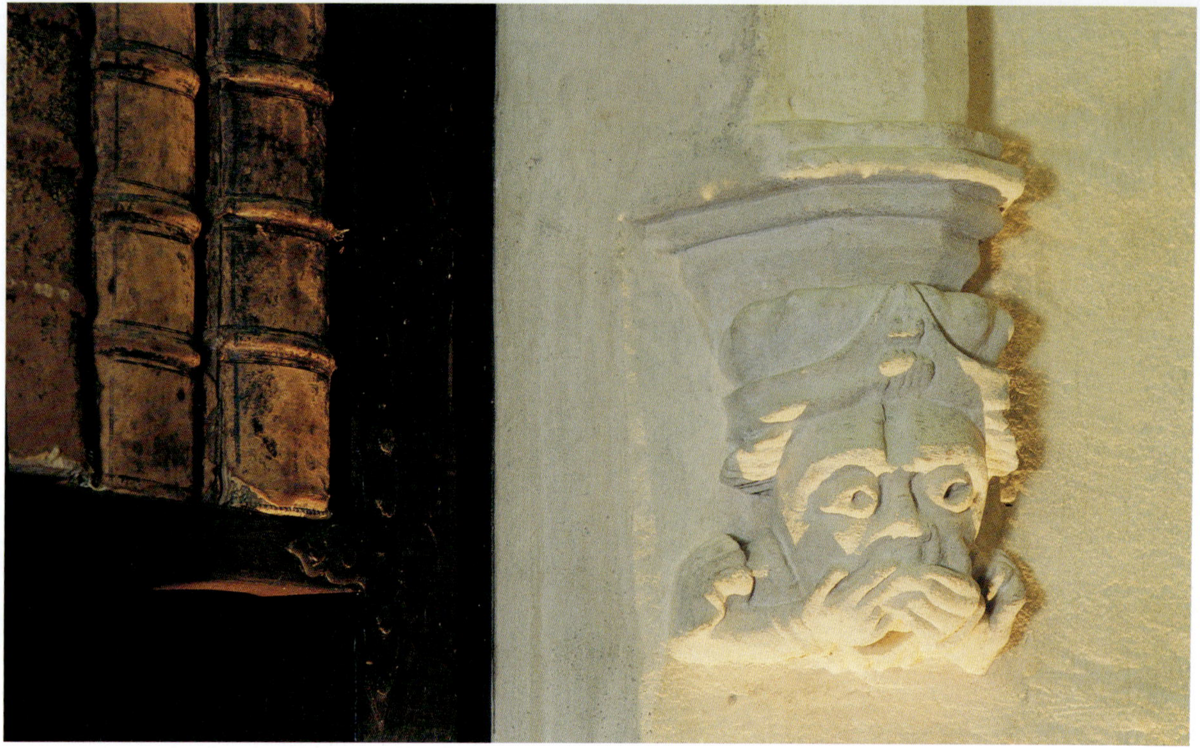

'Talk little and tread lightly' - Bodleian Library

Acknowledgements

Every effort has been made to secure permissions from copyright owners to use the extracts of text featured in this book. Any subsequent correspondence should be sent to Pitkin Publishing at the address at the front of this book.

page

15 (right) From *Highways and Byways in Oxfordshire* by Herbert Evans. Macmillan, 1905.

16 (left) From *Oxfordshire – County Books* by Joanna Cannan. Published by Hale, 1952. Reproduced by kind permission of the Estate of the late Joanna Cannan.

19 From *Oxford Observed* by Peter Snow. Published by John Murray, 1991. Reproduced by kind permission of John Murray (Publishers) Ltd.

21 (right) From *The Architecture of Southern England* by John Julius Norwich. Published by Macmillan, 1985. Reprinted by permission of the author.

23 (left) From *Oxfordshire* (in the series *The Buildings of England*) by Jennifer Sherwood and Nikolaus Pevsner. Published by Penguin, 1974. Reproduced by permission of Penguin Books Ltd.

26 (left) From *The King's England – Oxfordshire* by Arthur Mee. Published by Hodder & Stoughton 1949 and 1965. Reproduced by permission of Hodder & Stoughton Ltd.

29 From *Gaudy Night* by Dorothy L. Sayers. Published by Victor Gollancz, 1935. Reproduced by permission of David Higham Associates.

33 From *Sacheverell Sitwell's England* by Sacheverell Sitwell. Published by Little, Brown (Orbis) 1986. Reproduced by permission of David Higham Associates.

36 From *A Handy Guide to Oxford Specially Written for the Wounded* by C. R. L. Fletcher. Published by OUP, 1916. Reprinted by permission of OUP.

42 (left) From *The Oldest Music Room in Europe* by John Mee. Published by Bodley Head, 1911.

42 (right) From *Oxford Observed* by Thomas Sharp. Published by Country Life, 1952.

47 From The *Architecture of Southern England* by John Julius Norwich. Published by Macmillan, 1985. Reprinted by permission of the author.

51 From *Peel's England* by J. H. B. Peel. Published by David & Charles, 1977.

53 (right) From *A Handy Guide to Oxford specially written for the Wounded* by C. R. L. Fletcher. Published by OUP, 1916. Reprinted by permission of OUP.

54 (left) From *The Jewel that was Ours* by Colin Dexter. Published by Macmillan, 1991.

54 (right) From *Sinister Street* by Compton Mackenzie. Published by Macdonald, 1913. Reproduced by permission of The Society of Authors as the literary representatives of the Estate of Compton Mackenzie.

58 (left) From *Oxford Observed* by Thomas Sharp. Published by Country Life, 1952.

58 (right) From *Oxford* by Jan Morris. Published by Faber, 1965.

60 From *Portrait of Oxfordshire* by Christine G. Bloxham. Published by Hale, 1982.

61 From *Sinister Street* by Compton Mackenzie. Published by Macdonald, 1913. Reproduced by permission of The Society of Authors as the literary representatives of the Estate of Compton Mackenzie.

66 (left) From *The Golden Cross: Seven Centuries of an Oxford Inn* by E. A. Greening Lambourn. Published by Basil Blackwell, 1958.

68 (right) From *Portrait of Oxford* by Hal Cheetham. Published by Hale, 1971. © The Estate of J. H. Cheetham, 1971. Reprinted by permission of Campbell Thomson & McLaughlin.

71 From *Brideshead Revisited: The Sacred and Profane Memories of Captain Charles Ryder* by Evelyn Waugh (© Evelyn Waugh, 1945). Published by Chapman & Hall, 1945. Reprinted by permission of PFD on behalf of the Estate of Evelyn Waugh.

72 From *Oxford Observed* by Thomas Sharp. Published by Country Life, 1952.

74 (right) From *Oxford Renowned* by L. Rice-Oxley. Published by Methuen, 1925.

77 From *Buildings of Delight* by Alec Clifton-Taylor. Published by Victor Gollancz, 1986. Reprinted by permission of Victor Gollancz/Peter Crawley.

83 From *A Sort of Life* by Graham Greene. Published by Bodley Head. Reproduced by permission of David Higham Associates.

87 From *Follies, Grottoes and Garden Buildings* by Gwyn Headley and Wim Meulenkamp. Published by Aurum Press, 1999.

91 (right) From *Things Seen in Oxford* by Norman J. Davidson. Published by Seeley, Service, 1915.

100 (right) From *The End of the Chapter* by John Galsworthy. Published by Heinemann, 1935. Reproduced by permission of the Estate of John Galsworthy.

103 (left) From *The Silent Traveller in Oxford* by Chiang Yee. Published by Methuen, 1946. Reprinted by permission of Chian Fei Chiang.

109 From *Oxford* by Jan Morris. Published by Faber, 1965.

111 From *Oxford Renowned* by L. Rice-Oxley. Published by Methuen, 1925.

112 From *Oxford* by Jan Morris. Published by Faber, 1965.

114 (left) From *The King's England – Oxfordshire* by Arthur Mee. Published by Hodder & Stoughton, 1949 and 1965. Reproduced by permission of Hodder & Stoughton Ltd.

114 (right) From *The Silent Traveller* in Oxford by Chiang Yee. Published by Methuen, 1946. Reprinted by permission of Chian Fei Chiang.

Bibliography

Editions and dates in this bibliography are those of the items that have been examined. In some cases earlier editions have significant differences to those listed here.

Arnold, Frederick: *Oxford and Cambridge: their Memories and Associations.* Religious Tract Society, 1873.

Arnold, Matthew: *Essays in Criticism*, First Series, 1865 preface. Macmillan, 1907.

Bloxham, Christine G.: *Portrait of Oxfordshire.* Robert Hale, 1982.

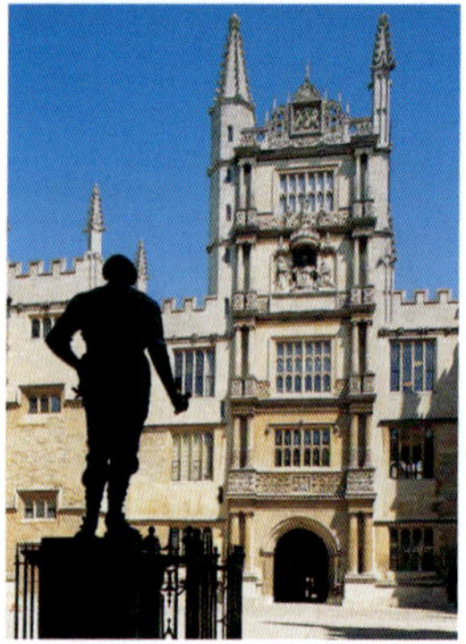

Tower of the Five Orders, Bodleian Library

Boswell, James: *The Life of Samuel Johnson, LL.D. Comprehending an Account of his Studies and Numerous Works 1776.* First published 1791, new edition Thomas Tegg etc., 1824.

Bourget, Paul: *Some Impressions of Oxford*, English version by M. C. Earrilow. Howard Wilford Bell, 1901.

Bradley, Edward: *The Adventures of Mr Verdant Green: an Oxford Freshman, by Cuthbert Bede,* B.A. Blackwood, 1853–57.

Burney, Fanny: *Diary and Letters of Madame d'Arblay, edited by her Niece.* Henry Colburn, 1854.

Byng, John: *Byng's Tours: the Journals of the Hon. John Byng, 1781–92*, edited by David Souden. Random Century, 1991.

Cannan, Joanna: *Oxfordshire (County Books).* Robert Hale, 1952.

Carlyle, Thomas: Letter to John Carlyle in J. A Froude: *Thomas Carlyle: A History of the First Forty Years of his Life, 1795–1835.* Longmans, Green, 1882.

Carroll, Lewis: *Alice's Adventures in Wonderland.* Macmillan, 1865.

Carroll, Lewis: *Through the Looking-Glass and What Alice Found There.* Macmillan, 1871.

Cheetham, Hal: *Portrait of Oxford.* Robert Hale, 1971.

Chiang Yee: *The Silent Traveller in Oxford.* 3rd edition, Methuen, 1946.

Clifton-Taylor, Alec: *Buildings of Delight*, edited by Denis Moriarty. Victor Gollancz in association with Peter Crawley. 1986.

Cook, Theodore Andrea: *The Sunlit Hours: a Record of Sport and Life.* Nisbet, 1925.

Davidson, Norman J.: *Things Seen in Oxford.* Seeley, Service, 1915.

Defoe, Daniel: *A Tour Through the Whole Island of Great Britain, 1724–26.* Dent, 1928.

Dexter, Colin: *The Jewel that was Ours.* Macmillan, 1991.

Evans, Herbert A.: *Highways and Byways in Oxford and the Cotswolds.* Macmillan, 1905.

Faber, F. W.: 'Aged Cities' in *The Minstrelsy of Isis: An Anthology Relating to Oxford and all Phases of Oxford Life*: selected and arranged by J. B. Firth. Chapman & Hall, 1908.

Faussett, Thomas: The letter, written to an absentee comrade at the close of term, is in W. Tuckwell: *Reminiscences of Oxford.* 2nd edition, Smith, Elder, 1907.

Fiennes, Celia: *The Illustrated Journeys of Celia Fiennes*, edited by Christopher Morris. Macdonald, 1982.

Flecker, James Elroy: *The Collected Poems of James Elroy Flecker*, edited with an introduction by J. C. Squire. Martin Flecker, 1916.

Fletcher, C. R. L.: *A Handy Guide to Oxford specially written for the Wounded.* Printed for the Author at the OUP, 1916.

Galsworthy, John: *The End of the Chapter.* Heinemann, 1935.

Gibbon, Edward: *Memoirs of My Life and Writings* in *The Miscellaneous Works of Edward Gibbon Esq., with Memoirs of His Life and Writings.* John Murray, 1814.

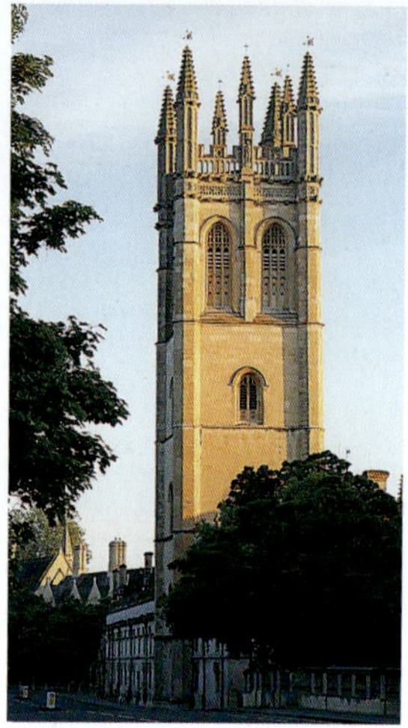

Morning sun on Magdalen Tower

Greene, Graham: *A Sort of Life.* Bodley Head, 1971.

A Handbook for Travellers in Berks, Bucks, and Oxfordshire, including a Particular Description of the University and City of Oxford. John Murray, 1860.

Hardy, Thomas: *Jude the Obscure.* Originally published 1896,

republished Penguin Books (Penguin Popular Classics), 1995.
Hawthorne, Nathaniel: *Passages from the English Notebooks of Nathaniel Hawthorne.* 2 vols, Strahan, 1870.
Hazlitt, William: *The Complete Works of William Hazlitt*, edited by P. P. Howe, Dent, 1931.
Headley, Gwyn and Meulenkamp, Wim: *Follies, Grottos and Garden Buildings.* Aurum Press, 1999.
How to See Oxford. The Pilot Press, 1928.
Hughes, Thomas: *Tom Brown at Oxford.* First published 1861, republished Macmillan, 1895.

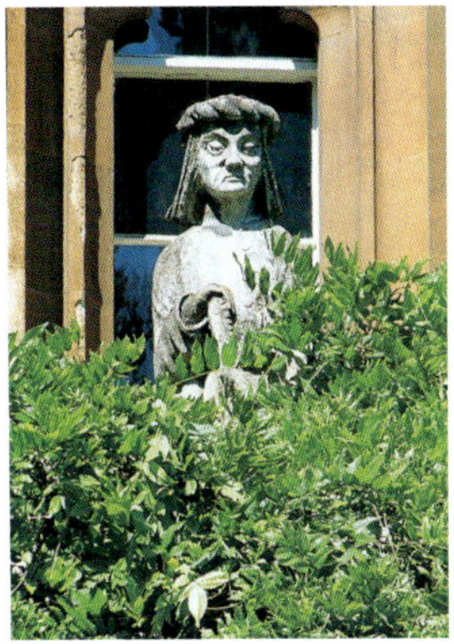

Figure in the cloister, Magdalen College

Ingram, James: Memorials of Oxford. John Henry Parker, 1837.
Kilvert, Francis: *Selections from the Diary of Rev Francis Kilvert, 14 May 1874–13 March 1879.* Chosen, edited and introduced by William Plommer. Jonathan Cape, 1940.
Lamb, Charles: *Essays of Elia, to which is added Letters, and Rosamund, a Tale.* Baudry's European Library, 1839.
Lambourn, E. A. Greening: *The Golden Cross: Seven Centuries of an Oxford Inn.* Oxford, Blackwell, 1948.
Lang, Andrew: *Oxford.* First published 1882, new edition, Seeley, 1906.
Mackenzie, Compton: *Sinister Street.* Macdonald, 1913.
Mee, Arthur: *The King's England – Oxfordshire.* Hodder & Stoughton, 1949.
Mee, John H.: *The Oldest Music Room In Europe: a Record of Eighteenth-Century Enterprise at Oxford.* John Lane, Bodley Head, 1911.
Morris, Jan: *Oxford.* Faber, first published 1965.
Müller, F. Max: *My Autobiography: a Fragment.* Longmans, Green, 1901.
Norwich, John Julius: *The Architecture of Southern England.* Macmillan, 1985.
Oxford. Oxford Visitors and Entertainments Committee, 1915.
Peel, J. H. B.: *Peel's England.* David & Charles, 1977.
Pepys, Samuel: *Diary and Correspondence of Samuel Pepys, F. R. S. Secretary to the Admiralty in the reign of Charles II and James II. With a Life and Notes by Richard, Lord Braybrooke.* Allen & Unwin, 1848–49, reprinted 1929.
Pictorial and Descriptive Guide to Oxford. Ward Lock, 1894.
Rice-Oxley, L.: *Oxford Renowned.* Methuen, 1925.
Sanders, N.: *The Complete English Traveller.* London, 1771.
Sayers, Dorothy L.: *Gaudy Night.* Gollancz, 1935.
Sharp, Thomas: *Oxford Observed.* Country Life, 1952.
Sherwood, Jennifer and Pevsner, Nikolaus: *Oxfordshire (The Buildings of England).* Penguin, 1974.
Sitwell, Sacheverell: *Sacheverell Sitwell's England*, edited by Michael Raeburn. Little, Brown (Orbis), 1986.
Snow, Peter: *Oxford Observed.* John Murray, 1991.
Southey, Robert: *Letters from England by Don Manuel Alvarez Espriella, Translated from the Spanish*, 2nd edition. Longman, Hurst, Rees and Orme, 1808.
Spencer, Nathaniel: *The Complete English Traveller: or a New Survey and Description of England.* J. Cooke, 1773.
Taunt, Henry W.: *Oxford: Illustrated by Camera and Pen.* Henry W. Taunt, 1911.
Tuckwell, W.: *Reminiscences of Oxford.* 2nd edition, Smith, Elder., 1907.
Walpole, Horace: *Horace Walpole's Correspondence*, edited by W. S. Lewis. Volume 35. OUP, 1973.
Waugh, Evelyn: *Brideshead Revisited: the Sacred and Profane Memories of Captain Charles Ryder.* Chapman & Hall, 1945.
Wilde, Oscar: *Review of Henry the Fourth*, Dramatic Review, May 23 1885.

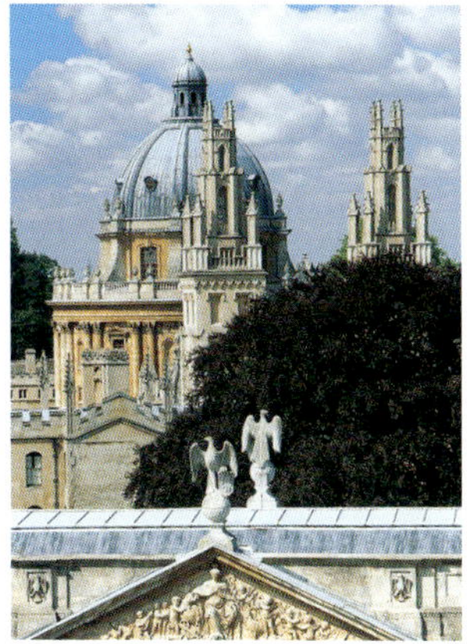

View from the library tower, St Edmund Hall

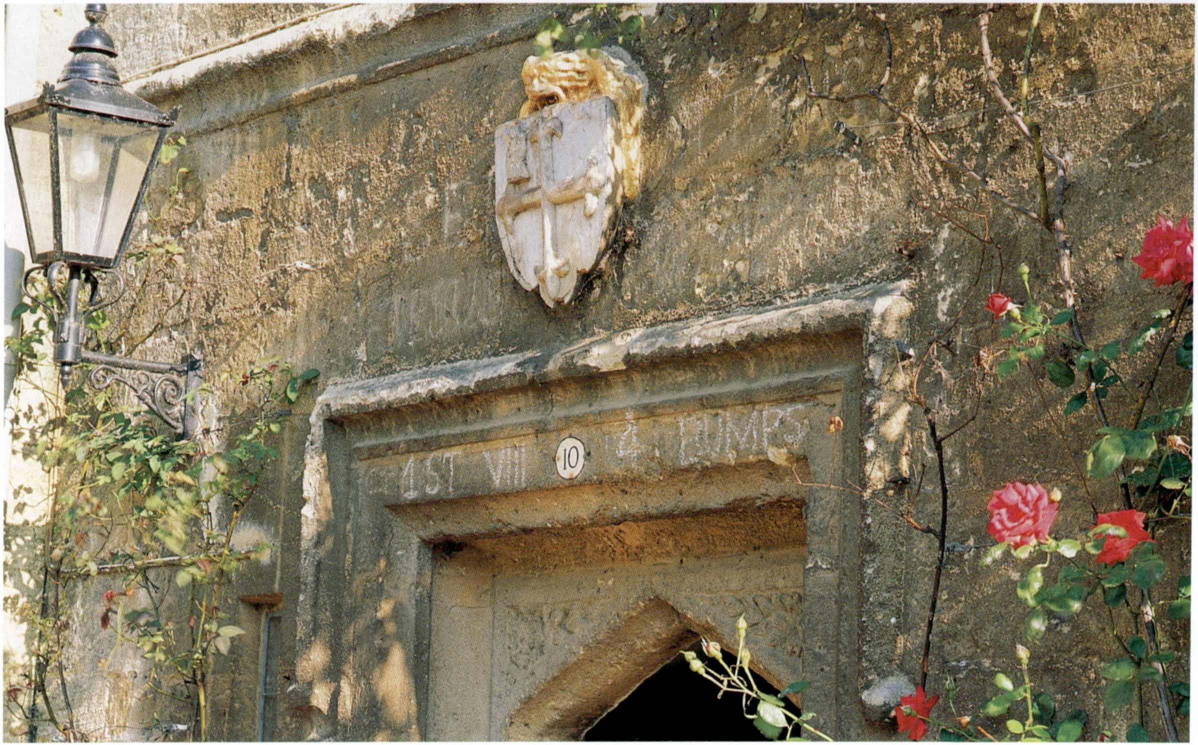

Worcester College, Main Quad

Index